Songs from the Stillness

Songs from the Stillness

JUSTIN KUIPER

RESOURCE *Publications* • Eugene, Oregon

SONGS FROM THE STILLNESS

Resource Publications
An Imprint of Wipf and Stock Publishers
199 W. 8th Ave., Suite 3
Eugene, OR 97401

www.wipfandstock.com

PAPERBACK ISBN: 979-8-3852-7246-4
HARDCOVER ISBN: 979-8-3852-7247-1
EBOOK ISBN: 979-8-3852-7248-8

VERSION NUMBER 01/19/26

To the poets.

Contents

Preface

As a college student, stillness can be very hard to find. I am constantly inundated by the rush of classes and activities and athletics. My phone screen blazes with a firestorm of notifications, and my inbox persistently demands my attention. Yet in the wooden pews on a Sunday morning or in the packed-out chapel on Hope College's chapel three times a week—those unexpected clefts in the hills of time in which the world finally quiets from its bustling—I am reminded again that stillness is perhaps one of the most overlooked aspects of the Christian life. This book was born out of that realization.

Songs From the Stillness is a collection of 365 short poems written everyday between my senior year of high school and the dawn of my freshman year of college. In this book, I explore the themes of stillness, faith, creation, and ultimately, the hope that all things might one day be made new. Most of these daily poems stand on their own, while others bleed into the next day. Most are a short five lines in length, others may take up half a page, and all are marked with the time stamp at which the poem was written. This variation in style, set beside the particularity of time, is meant to capture both the ever-changing nature of our lives, and the rhythms that guide us day to day. Some days, our hope soars like the eagle and we are taken aback by the sheer beauty of the world. Yet sometimes—oftentimes—the words are muffled and slow in their coming. This collection of poems, therefore, is meant to be a careful companion on all of those days. A hymnal of thanks when the world is right and a friend in lament when all hope seems lost.

There are three things I hope to accomplish through this book. Firstly, I want to train my heart and the hearts of you, my readers, to see the holiness in the ordinary. If all things came into being from the lips of God, then all things, in their own measure, must bear a trace of holiness—even those things often considered too mundane to write about. Perhaps it is in the mundane most of all in which the presence of God shines the clearest if we have the eyes to see it. Secondly, I see these poems as a striving after of the heart of God. The God of the Scriptures, after all, does not dwell in the tempest, or the earthquake, or the fire, but rather in the gentlest of breezes; a breeze so quiet that we must enter fully in if we hope to catch a glimpse of our Maker there (1 Kings 19:11–13). And finally, this book is meant to push back against a world that too often values busyness over stillness. This is a stark misalignment of priorities, and its foul fruit is evident all around us: in wars and political polarization and health crises and all other proofs of our exile from Eden. Many of the poems in this book deal with these themes, unto the ultimate hope that we might all, as Wendell Berry wrote, "come into the peace of wild things" and reassess which things are truly and eternally important.

Concisely, I see the purpose of *Songs From the Stillness* in this way: it is a signpost standing in the midst of our crazy, free-wheeling world to direct the heart back toward the sacrament of stillness, to the Kingdom ever hinting around the corners of creation, and to the God himself who takes up dwelling in the gentle whisper and invites us in to join him there in the great secret. And if somehow you are able to touch the hem of this glorious Maker through this book in the stillness between lines, then my job is done.

So, if you come to find this book in your hands, then my prayer is that it points you to the stillness at the heart of things and prompts you to pursue it in all your little spheres of influence. And most of all, to *see*. The ground still echoes with holiness, if only you'll quiet yourself. The woods still shiver with magic, if only you'll look. The wind still carries the fragrance of Eden, if only you'll breathe. Strive and yearn and hope and dream and follow our rambling Maker further up and further in where, upon the borderlands of the cosmos, Christ himself stands to shout over the shoulders of time, "Behold! I am making all things new!"

The stories, after all, are true.

—Justin Kuiper

I

January

JANUARY 1 10:52 AM

Come into the holy place, where every whisper is praise,
come and sit in the drenching peace of this silence.
For the world around us is glimmering with promises
that we only notice when we are still. So, join me on this sojourn
and we may find things we didn't dare to imagine.

JANUARY 2 10:11 AM

Oh Maker of Years and Great Timekeeper of Heaven, let me, by your gracious
will, be guided this new year by the animating breath of your Holy Ghost. You gave me life,
and thus, it is yours. In the year to come, help me to be mindful of the shortness of
my own life and therefore more aware of you and the beauty that imbues all things.
For indeed, there is beauty, if only I open my eyes to see it.

JANUARY 3 11:12 AM

To all the authors who had the courage to take up a sword and face their dragons,

who built the towering castle turrets, who made the ships and wove their captains.

To all the authors who tilled the earth and planted seeds within the ground,

who stoked red fire upon the hearth and saw veiled magic in the clouds.

To all the authors who roamed the forest and sunk their feet into the grass,

who listened to an unseen chorus, who saw beyond the looking glass.

To all the authors I wish I'd known, who painted colors in the water,

who chiseled beauty from the stone, you've made me too into an author.

JANUARY 4 12:05 PM

A tree is not merely a resource to be cultivated to further the crawl of

industry. A tree is a timeless giant, a solemn Ent, a sentry over memory,

a paragon of purity as it drinks light from the clouds and

pulls water from sunken pools. A tree, so long passed by and ignored, might

even be the distant descendent of the Tree in the Garden.

A tree has fragments of Eden in its leaves.

JANUARY 5 10:57 AM

Let my art, oh Lord, my creative works, billow with fresh sweetness as of
morning dew. May they, like a bridge founded by and rooted deep in the soil of
story, span from heaven to earth, from earth to heaven.
Guide my poet's pen to lend shape to the form of unknown things,
and give to unseen glories a home among us here.

JANUARY 6 11:45 AM

There have been moments in my life in which the veil felt so thin that the glory of the quickly nearing Kingdom seemed at once to invade with the sweet fragrance of music and story and poetry and song.
But today I stand in a country where the veil is so dense, so calloused by the pummeling
of the world. Can you, oh Christ, invade even here? Could this be a windowsill into that far country?

JANUARY 7 5:26 PM

Have you ever wished you could speak with trees, or soar with the stars in
the gloaming heights? Have you ever longed to sing with birds, or sleep in the
woods next to streams of light? Have you ever dreamed of wandering forever through
pastures and hills and cliffs and snow? Have you ever felt like you heard a low
whisper, only to wonder where e'er did it go?
The stories, dear child, the stories are true.

JANUARY 8 5:03 PM

Every temptation that torments me, every stone that makes me stumble, every pitfall I wander headlong into, every sorry facade dripping like

poisoned honey from sugared lips will one day

be rent to pieces by the King of Love. But until that glorious morn,

help me to stand and stand and stand though bloodied my soul may be.

JANUARY 9 12:14 PM

The sun has emerged this afternoon for the first time in weeks.

I feel that I have never witnessed such a suffusion of light.

And the thought crosses my mind that just as this sudden awakening of

flowing gold was made more beautiful by the darkness that bookended it, so the

many sorrows we endure here may one day be seen full and lovely in the light of the Son.

JANUARY 10 10:49 AM

My heart: a shattered castle surrounded by crumbling walls.

They keep the dark marauder away from these rough, winding roads,

but they too often admit a black-cloaked whisper of thought that disguises

itself as a merchant or a benevolent charlatan who promises joy to my ruinous castle.

But he's already wrecked one city before like mine: a garden kingdom rife with deathly fruit.

JANUARY 11 11:00 AM

There is a dingy, backstreet tavern, hung about with sour-smelling smoke
from a hundred cigarettes and the fumes of a thousand meals hastily and sloppily thrown together.
The reek of cheap ale strangles the air and it moves leadenly across a floor dirtied
with the refuse of a hundred worn sneakers. There are prostitutes here and
druggies and tormented souls in the throes of addiction; there are single mothers
trying to swamp trauma with alcohol and old, earthy folks who have long been at odds with the world.
This is the lair of criminals and delinquents, of promiscuity and
violence; the heart cry of these hundred wrecked souls, if it could be gathered and condensed down into
sound would bring tears rushing to your eyes.
There is a man who sits alone in the dark corner of the tavern.
He is out of place, to be sure, but the scars arrayed across his deprived body tell this
assembly of tattered women and twisted men that he is one of them. He is not
afraid of this rough and tumble mass of rugged humanity; for he has tasted deeply the
full cruelty of the world outside the tavern, and he chooses to sit
among them and tell the stories of his own scars.

JANUARY 12 2:15 PM

God, I've tried so hard to find words to write,
I've tried to use this wonderful gift, but the words
are so stuck and the spigot run dry, yet

help me to see you are bigger than this.
Because you, in the end, are the most wonderful gift.

JANUARY 13 4:26 PM

She is a living behemoth, a somber giantess, an ageless sage. The chaplet of ages
rests upon her thorny brow, the tunic of quaking leaves and the girdle of
flowered vines cloaks her ringed bones and enshrouds her whispered secrets.
A perfume of lavender fringes her star-sprinkled hair, and she
drinks from the sunken pools of the woods and waters. She is a tree.

JANUARY 14 9:34 AM

The rising sun speckles the lawn. A vat of blistering gold behind the horizon
sends burning rivulets into the wood and they bubble and flow,
searching for avenues through the tightly woven tree line. The few rogue
brands that steal past those watchful sentries repose yellow-gold
on the frosty green of the lawn and still the sun pushes higher and higher.

JANUARY 15 5:24 PM

And now the sun begins to sink below the distant west
like a glowing sphere of gold that rained from the heavens and into the sea.

The waters above steam and smoke, caught up in a fury of burning eddies
and seething currents; a chariot of light riding swiftly away to brighten
whatever lands lay beyond our tilting world.

JANUARY 16 3:30 PM

Raindrops slide down the window pane, distorting
the stormy outdoors. The sky is weeping as I stare at
it from behind this rain-slicked glass; weeping at who it sees: an
image-bearer, a priest of the garden kingdom who is just as distorted
as the view through this window. It sees a boy who
drips from his lashes with mud.

JANUARY 17 3:09 PM

The wheels of my mind turn day and night, nudged along by the rivers
of plot and hope and story. I yearn to finish this book—a thing I both adore
and abhor and yet each time I've sat down to write lately, the wheels
suddenly grind to an inconvenient halt. If anything, there's a slow, languid dripping
of words, but other than that, it simply won't come. Writer's block is real, folks.

JANUARY 18 9:03 AM

The thunder of water. It echoes on far slopes and snowy shires rasped by wind

and down through the ages: the soil, the shrugging stones, the mist-veiled pine needles,

all hear and remember. They tremble. It pours over the rim of the cliff side,

a saucer of milk tipped and spilled in the pines above, and then it roars.

Blades of water carve veins in the stone. Atom-fine mist filters like motes of

falling frost. So violent, so good, as if the Maker of these mountains must be terrible

enough to quiver the knees, yet beautiful enough to make the heart weep like

firs dripping after-rain. And the stream winds away through the laurels,

Milk-moon blue: the thunder's lifeblood

JANUARY 19 4:47 PM

I feel sometimes like a hobbit holed up in the ground, gazing out at the

same wending roads round the same yellow-green corner. But there's a

Tookishness in me also; I long to see mountains, Gandalf, and go on some

high adventure to a far country. I long for the mountains while I am yet in the hills,

and the song of the journey bids me ever on. Yet for now, I will be content with the

glow of home, and the quests I find merely in the pages of books.

JANUARY 20 4:07 PM

Trees: mighty pillars of sinew and wood rising to uphold the sky.
Sky: a roof like that of a king's great hall, swirling with blue and white and gray.
Ground: a floor green and carpeted lushly upon which little worshippers bound.
Garden: fruit from soil offered as pleasing gifts unto the High King.
Creation is a temple, and the rabbits like tiny priests.

JANUARY 21 2:32 PM

There's a glaze of ice on the trees today and they stand like water reeds
stiff and cold by the breath of a stream long frozen by winter.
The slush on the back porch crunches like autumn leaves beneath
my feet as the air—crisp and cold and keen as a silver needle—moves
around me like the currents of a stream long held in the enchantment of spring.

JANUARY 22 5:24 PM

I stand alone on this shattered ground: the broken knolls of my heart.
Tendrils of black smoke rise sickly here from charred cities inhabited by
fractured women and splintered men. Foul water runs in oily rivulets through
this gouged and divot-ridden land, and I squat hunched on my heels, bruised and
bloody, surveying it all with weary eyes.
It feels like this heart is at war sometimes, and it's all I can do not to fall.

JANUARY 23 4:18 PM

Silence. Stillness. Quiet. The trees know these words intimately. They drink
of the water and breathe in the sun: growing, ever growing, fattening
a ring each year, so the scientists say. Their every sighing movement a
burst of hushed praise, or so the poets say.
Can you hear them budding? When I am still—truly still—I sometimes think I can. And this
is what the trees teach us: to be silent and still and quiet and see the world. Truly See.

JANUARY 24 1:45 PM

The lords of the mountain stone sigh icicled breath upon the high ridges
where not even the pines dare to whisper. Beads of water spray from the
lips of grandfather falls: liquid light in the veins of bluebells drawn from
petals like soul-stones, low, bone-weary aches in the dragon-caverns of the mountain.
All becomes crystal in the mountain lord's orbiting iris, an ever-winter
on the shoulder of the ridge. The glacier creeps. The glacier weeps.
Tears wrinkle the sandstone to furrows, and they fall dripping, sighing, dream-like
into a basin; melted sapphires lapping at the shore like a cat's tongue at milk
until the weeping glacier one day spills the basin over
and its soul-melting grief runs into the pine-strewn valleys
and crowns the wood with wands of ice.

JANUARY 25 6:00 PM

The glacier is laid on the mountainsides like a wolf skin, fog-blue and melting
and bristling along the hackles with ice. I wonder, as I mark my footfalls in this ancient
snow, what secrets lie hidden in its fathomless deeps? What twisted ruins, what
misplaced tales? What trees slowly sundered from the moss by its pensive,
eldritch crawl? What snow-pearled bones of creatures older than memory?
Would that I could burrow down, down into pillars of ice where lie entombed
the frozen fallen, to streams that slipped from the world unnoticed
and ancient wells long forgotten, then deeper still. Down to ice older than Abraham,
to frosts that were already gray with age on the stone when thunder fell on
Sinai. And there, I would lie down with the old things and sleep.

JANUARY 26 1:43 PM

The doors holding the snow back have been heaved open by angelic gatekeepers
and all I see as I look out my window is a landscape touched by ice.
It falls as free and as wild as unfettered horses tossing their heads in wide pasture;
it seems there should be some proclamation of its whimsical existence, yet it swirls
down utterly silent, like, perhaps the love of God:
fierce and raging, yet soft as a dream as it settles upon the winter-worn soul.

JANUARY 27 8:24 AM

I awoke this morning to color as I stepped outdoors
and beheld another world. The grass was pearled by a
sea of pale crystals and the trees stood tall and still against the sky.
The sky! As brightly gold as an alchemist's workbench, the sun like a sliver
of fruit on the silver horizon; the heads of the trees golden, their knees swaddled in shadow.

JANUARY 28 10:06 AM

Keep my eyes open, oh Lord, each and every day.
For if beauty is truly what I'm after in these poems, it's here all around me
to see. But the beauty is shy and silent amid the clamor and
bustle of life, so to find it, we must all lift up our eyes and for once be truly
still. Help me, great Weaver of Beauty, to see your face in everything!

JANUARY 29 10:27 AM

I am living a fairy tale. I am surrounded by characters penned into being
by the same Author who wrote the myths of creation and redemption and
snowfall into the pages of the sky. And all these things—the fairies, the snowfall,
and the characters—foreshadow the sudden, joyful twist
in which the dawn will blaze forth and our hearts shall burst with fire.

JANUARY 30 8:48 AM

Each branch is lined with snow and ice that catches the color
of daybreak. Faint, breathy gold; pale, rosy white;
deep, teary-eyed blue; soft, gentle pink. These fall in
bands across the expanse of snow like wands of life
and light and beauty through a land drenched in wonder.

JANUARY 31 5:56 PM

So often have I written about sunsets that now I begin to
run short on words. But they so enthrall me, these gleaming
envelopes folded around the King's flowing script:
the white clouds turning over like parchment, the melting gold burning
a seal into the sky and the vibrant red a reminder of blood once spilled for me.

II

February

FEBRUARY 1 5:01 PM

A million shining crystals on a thousand blades of grass,
speckled by a myriad of pencil-stroke shadows from the hundred silent trees.
It's as white as Narnia, as a dove's soft breast, as a bride's
wedding gown. And the sky is as blue as a winking pond,
as a swollen blueberry bush, as a golden irised eye.

FEBRUARY 2 9:52 PM

The house is quiet and it settles around me like an old friend by a warm
hearth who has beheld much of my life and now cheerfully walks through it
alongside me. This silence is sweet, like an unexpected calm descending after
a winter storm. And as night falls as a curtain outside,
I finish my writing and slowly make my way to books and bed.

FEBRUARY 3 8:37 PM

A candle: flickering, dancing, a tongue of flame like Pentecost
accosting this bending wick. Scents of cinnamon and apple
and nutmeg and autumn; a purple-blue body crowned by a chaplet
of liquid gold—feathered and brushed by the air moving
slowly around. A light for this room, a warmth on my hands.

FEBRUARY 4 9:50 AM

The lake has frozen along the beach in great rises and
hummocks of snow and ice. Beyond, far beyond, the western
horizon
gleams gold and pink and red like the throat of an angry dragon
and the ice catches the color and lifts its own rosy lips in a smile.
It's like an alien landscape, like another world here on earth.

FEBRUARY 5 10:59 AM

There's an ache within me when I look outside and see the sky
teeming with flurries of snow. There's a longing I carry deep in
my bones when I hear a strain of music or read from a book.
There's a yearning inside that I can give no name except:
Country I've Never Visited, Flower I've Never Smelled, Story I've
Never Heard.

FEBRUARY 6 5:07 PM

Westward sails the golden sun and Holland's hills are crowned
with amber. And I remember as this song plays on the radio,
that I once prayed in this lakeside town that you would make it

a Promised Land. I have yet to see it, Lord; even so, as the sun sinks away,
I remember your goodness and trust in your grace.

FEBRUARY 7 11:15 AM

Every time I sit down to write, my head is filled with a gallery of voices:
"Do this and not that. Do that and not this. Who are you really?
You have nothing to say. Why, you can scarcely even write.
Nobody will like this. Nobody likes *you*." And these voices eddy madly through
my head and it's so hard sometimes to disbelieve what they said.

FEBRUARY 8 2:10 PM

I was writing just a moment ago: a dialogue between the King and a character
broken by shame littering his past. And I felt as if the Lord were bidding me
to pay attention; that the words I was putting to page and into the King's mouth
are the same words he has been trying to tell me for years on end:
that I am still loved and can never manage to outrun His grace.

FEBRUARY 9 6:34 PM

The peace of silence and the silence of still; still I long for it,
yet rarely is it found. The world around me buzzes and beeps and
clatters and clangs and spins and sputters and sparks; it is so hard to find

that moment within moments when all things grind grandly to a halt
and the vast, undergirding still is allowed to well untroubled from the ground.

FEBRUARY 10 10:21 AM

The snow has gone away, away; the snows have gone away.
And now instead of white and pale, the earth is fresh and
green again. The sky has shed its skin of gray and glitters
a crystalline, clear-eyed blue and the trees sway gladly in this frigid breeze.
The snow has gone away, away; the snows have gone away.

FEBRUARY 11 5:45 PM

It's on days like this when the sky is bright and the sun casts its riches o'er
the winter-green world that I feel like I'm somehow on the edge of something
impossibly holy and majestic, yet I can only look in from outside. How I long for the day when
every evening is like this, when I'm no longer an imposter, but rather in on the great secret:
a note in the far-off song, a character in the winding script of glory.

FEBRUARY 12 4:46 PM

Oh that my faith were as mighty as legends: as everlasting
as a redwood oak, or the jutting knee of a sea-battered cliff, or the

ironwood sides of a ship's hull, or a story resisting the pull of centuries past.
And yet, too often, my faith is an autumn leaf: fallen and brown,
blown about by the whims of the wind, by the currents of the world.

FEBRUARY 13 6:10 PM

The fire has died a little and now it ebbs fully away.
Father Sun dips below the curtains of Mother Sky but the afterglow
of that great, heaven-bound fire is still enough to read by. The cold nips
at my bare fingers and I'm thinking that gloves wouldn't have been amiss,
but I really couldn't care less here in this peace of wild things.

FEBRUARY 14 10:09 AM

How oft do I live my life and yet never truly live it?
I walk with my eyes down, not up to marvel at sun and stars,
nor do I live as if each day were a miracle, a marvel that points
to the nearing Kingdom. The saints and poets see it sometimes, yet rarely do I. Let
me, oh merciful God, at last lift my head that I might follow the sun and soar with the stars.

FEBRUARY 15 5:06 PM

Old man mountain. He looms sternly over the ebbing lake. The cliffs echo under
the rumbling of his breast. On his gnarled brow, stones have cracked and

trees have felled and wolves have wailed at the waxen moon, yet the old man remained.

We walk about his pine-girdled waist and pass unseen into his hoary beard of

evergreen and auburn. The footpath winds before me like a twine laid upon the hills,

and the earth is muffled by a russet mead of pine needles. Does the old man

know we walk here? Does he feel our feet pattering, squirreling between his

shoulder blades? Or has his spine become too weathered in this eon-old sleep to notice?

But dreaming or waking, he bids us ascend. Dew drips from the pines like falling magnets and

we are drawn ever upward on the mountain's twisting vertebrae to its great, rocky crown.

FEBRUARY 16 9:40 AM

Chinks of gild in the slate of clouds; breaches of blue

in the distant heights; fields of white on this snowy lawn;

a garland of lights all green and gold; a case of old books every shade;

a carpet of cream; a bed of almond; a floor of

hickory; a guitar of coffee; a desk of mahogany; a world of color.

FEBRUARY 17 5:33 PM

Why is it so hard to lift our weary heads from all the scattered

entanglements about us and simply delight in this creation that

whirs the world with glory? Why is it so easy to become snarled in the

crosshairs of voices that grumble and ooze, yet not recognize
how the rot in our hearts echoes louder than even the noise about us?

FEBRUARY 18 1:24 PM

The hills, like a stern brow, stretch away into the trees.
The trees: like staves laid and laden with shadows across this
expanse of snow. Snow: so smooth and pure and white—undisturbed
by the pattering footfalls of woodland creatures—saving these
faint prints left by a rabbit beside the screen door.

FEBRUARY 19 10:31 AM

To sit and look at wind-blown snow allows me to see, as through
a veil, the glory undergirding all things. The glory of work and
rest and holy Sabbath. To sit and look at a lawn of white speckled
by the thin shadows of winter-worn trees reminds a deep sanctuary of
my soul that an ancient garden ever lingers around the fringes of memory.

FEBRUARY 20 10:25 PM

The snow recedes from a sloping brow, from a sloping brow
of green. And the cold retreats to the misty heights, to the misty heights
of ice. Just as one day, this world will fade, this world will fade into
wonder. And the ice and snow will melt away, will recede again, then
melt away into the dew and cool of Eden's spring, of Eden's spring refreshed.

FEBRUARY 21 10:04 AM

The high vaults of winter have been riven by a hairline breach
that heavenly courtiers hurry desperately to patch. But they cannot
keep out the slow whisper of snowfall that descends now around my
home. The forecasters have predicted that those courtiers will not
patch
the rift in time—we will have a blizzard tomorrow. Perhaps they
need some duck tape.

FEBRUARY 22 10:51 AM

The grass is glazed with sugar, the grill is white with frost,
the sky is choked with clouds, the breeze is chill and soft.
The trees are still as sentries, the bracken bends and breaks,
the winter storm is coming from beyond the wrathful lake.
The icy gale descending upon our berth and bower,
a whirling, whining chaos, a wind-blown winter flower.

FEBRUARY 23 4:00 PM

A sheath of ice engulfs the lawn. I look out the window and am
stricken with the uncanny sensation that I am on a ship braving
wild,
Arctic seas. All is frozen and gray in the grip of winter's thrall.
The sun glistens off the surface of the ice fields and sends
shards of golden light spiraling into this ship: into this house, into
my heart.

FEBRUARY 24 9:07 AM

Oh Lord, I try to be brave, but my heart is cleft with fiery brands of fear. I stand alone on the vast chasm of the rest of my life and all I can see in the void is a swirling, gray emptiness that divulges nothing. I'm scared to take that leap, scared that I might lose myself in the midst of that pale, roiling madness. And yet, if you are there, oh Lord, then I feel that I must leap and encounter the wings of your goodness when my feet have left ground.

FEBRUARY 25 4:50 PM

Perhaps the sky is an ocean and we live far underwater—the breeze like soft currents, these trees like waterweed—and the moon is naught but a glimpse of a higher land that we can only swim up to with the right sort of ship. Perhaps when the sun hangs by a thread and paints the blue of the sky with gold, it really is sinking away into the upper seas and the simmering reds and purples are the steam of that great burning. We can always imagine.

FEBRUARY 26 4:57 PM

I have yet to witness a perfect day; some, like this one, seem to draw close—when the hills remember what it means to be green and the skies wick ablaze in a raiment of blue, when the winds are cool and green,

when birds fill the afternoon air with wreathes of song—yet it is not. All things
seem to groan as they wait for that final Sabbath morn to dawn.

FEBRUARY 27 10:59 AM

Yesterday was as green as an apple in spring. Today is gray as the havens,
but neither to me is more beautiful than the other. Sun or rain is all
the same: the world straining in its limited power to rehearse that dawn
that once surged over the hills of Eden—the dawn bodied and embodied by the Dawn
itself. This rainfall could, I suppose, be tears, but couldn't it also be drops of yearning
falling to the earth and begging it to grow again that lost tree of life?

FEBRUARY 28 9:49 AM

The snows begin to withdraw from my windowsill like the month of February
now in its final day (unless, of course, it's a Leap Year—which I do not have a poem for!).
The trees outside stand tall like pillars against the cloud-teeming steeps,
and I wonder how many winters these elemental giants
have weathered and how many more they'll see after I have gone.

III

March

MARCH 1 9:57 AM

The boat motors along over turquoise deeps and waves murmur good-naturedly
against the hull. I imagine mermaids peering up from frigid depths where castles of ice
raised on the far, barren belly of the lake teem with couriers of lake trout
and where sunken cities and the skeletons of old, grizzled bears signpost toward the king
of the lake. The ancients rowed these waters, they say. Leaf-light canoes of deer hide
stretched over mighty pine timbers that cut across the pitted moon of the forest's scalp.
Can you see them? They named this place "spirit water"; a place thinner than skin in which
the divine stooped and rested a finger upon the world. And every-where I see it.

Fingerprints in a ripple of water. Laughter in the fog climbing off the lake.

Peace as still as a water reed.

MARCH 2 12:46 PM

Two chambers in my soul war tirelessly against the other member.

On the left, there's a wretched hall filled with flesh, ruptured by sores of desire.

On the right, a gilded castle of liquid light that pours upon my heart from the Maker's

laughing lips. In my head, I long for right, I yearn for the garden temple lost,

and yet, often I stray from the path and find myself hopelessly entangled.

MARCH 3 12:17 PM

Cars buzz along these dusty freeways like a horde of black insects crawling along toward whatever worries and destinations rule their shining metal minds. The sky gazes down, weeping for four-wheeled messiahs that line our streets without a glimpse outward and upward to a sweet promise that will end their polluting exhalations, their foul exhausts.

MARCH 4 1:52 PM

I write today on the open road. Walls of turf line the highway,

undulating like waves laden with cattails and shaking ferns and slumbering

trees atop this ever-shifting crust of earth. And away

between two steep-shouldered knolls, I see a gossamer gleam of water
winking like a gentle eye that roves the world of wonder around it.

MARCH 5 9:40 AM

Each morning, all is silent. It's as if a wheel so long employed in churning the river over its wooden spokes, comes, for a moment, to partake of Sabbath sleep. The wheel stills and lingers in the green of the wood. I sense that this place is etched with the fingerprints of the ones who dwell
here and I wonder if my heart might be the same: riven through with the love
of the Spirit who rambles like a whisper across these inward halls.

MARCH 6 3:09 PM

There are places that simply feel right, that have somehow been able to remember the sacred threads that wove them together and scorn that dark desecration that creeps steadily over every good, truth-bearing
thing. For me, that place is a tree leaning over Quincy Street.
It stands at the intersection of brown and green—itself a pure, long-limbed
white, as if the dryad within is preparing to wed the lord of springtime.

MARCH 7 9:15 AM

Your presence, oh Lord, hangs heavy over this chapel of creation through which I now walk. And it is here that I lay down

my worries and fears at the altar stone of wildness. How small and passing they seem in the moss! They are but a blink, a mote of dust falling before
your light. I am reminded that this breeze has hushed through the winter bracken for centuries and the trees have fattened since by hundreds
of rings and the springs that feed this river have done so for ages. And you smiled and beheld it all since before I even opened my eyes.

MARCH 8 4:02 PM

Springtide has broken over the world and the hillsides summon green into its roots. The trees are dressed in whispers of red, ready at once to burst and bloom. After the long, pale winter, creation has banded together to usher in warmth after the cold,
calm after the storm, and dawn after the dark.

MARCH 9 2:29 PM

My heart is pained and calloused with cataracts of ice that run like needles through my veins. I feel so broken, so profane, so swallowed
by shame, and I long to be made whole. The sorrows here are nothing to the joys
yet to come, I know, but the wandering is so real, so keen and sharp. I yearn for your
Kingdom, my God, to descend among these furrows and turn them to art.

MARCH 10 10:01 AM

Each plant is crowned by a cap of snow, each branch mantled as
with a wintry sheath. And still it lazily drips from the heavens like
a spigot allowed to leak today over the lakes and the land.
A patchwork of white: it's all I see when I look out the window—white
like pearls, white like lambs, white like petals, the white of snow.

MARCH 11 2:38 PM

Open my eyes, remove these stiffened scales that I might see into the
life of things and write what can only be described as billows of water-rushed
color. Guide my steps and light my path, that I might sneak past the watchful
dragons of misbegotten reason and smuggle light from Fairyland into this seething
darkness—light that might slowly transfigure our world into your beauty and image.

MARCH 12 10:35 AM

A prism of clear crystal held up to the sun. The light streams
through and shatters into refracted pieces. Shards of
shades spray on the pavement below. Those shades aren't the light, nor the
prism, but rather an incarnation of that falling light. That is
what fairy stories are: an utterance of beyond, a glimpse beyond the veil.

MARCH 13 10:58 AM

How I wish my heart was still and restful, clear-eyed and ready to marvel at the world and the Maker who crafted it. I wish that my heart was like a sloping hillside drenched in snow: crackle-crisp and breathless,
soothing to spirit, still as a whisper, white as clean linen,
fresh as an un-worn garment, innocent as a child's song.

MARCH 14 10:19 AM

I sat last night in the cheery afterglow cast by candles and garland lights,
and I wept over a book resting in my hands. An ache speared through my chest as I read that final word and I yearned profoundly for it to
be true. And it seemed that the great Storyteller opened up a window through which rumors passed of my native country and truest home.

MARCH 15 11:33 AM

Help me, Father, to think on what is holy and good and perfect and beautiful and true, to consider the birds of the air and the flowers in
the field and the trees laced with breeze and the sky burning blue. My time is fleeting—this I know, and yet how often do I fail to truly be still?
How often do I worship at the altar of self and fail to see you?

MARCH 16 9:35 AM

A glow of yellow behind the trees, like a vat of melted gold spilled out upon
the earth, and the razor-thin lip of snow basks in that cheery shadow.
A sphere of dancing flame toes the horizon's needle edge.
Higher and higher it soars into the depths of high heaven. An eruption
of light—a river of gold—daylight and dawn have broken o'er the world!

MARCH 17 8:28 AM

Each morning is new and baptized: baptized by a fount of wonder like
a fresh canvas stretching from the mind of God. Today, the canvas
is a patchwork of green: evergreen grass speckled with hints of
moss. Each tree is draped with a cloak of lichen brought about by last night's
rain. Even the air smells faintly green, as if spring were singing from these waking hills.

MARCH 18 11:01 AM

A little pond in the woods, gathered like wisping mist between
three shallow hills, is half-frozen today in the whistling cold.
The driving flurry of snowfall dapples it white like the back of
a rabbit, or the cloudy eyes of a blind woodland creature.
A little pond in the woods: in spring a watering-hole; in winter, a frosty gravestone.

MARCH 19 8:10 PM

Come step outside with me, come and be still with me,
come watch the firmament blaze away the clouds with me.
Come stand in this gloaming, this afterglow in which
the trees and grass are transfigured rose-gold. Come rest in awe
under that darkening sky and watch as one by one, the stars wake in the deep.

MARCH 20 10:30 PM

The moon rises. A pearl-pale crescent perched endlessly in the heavens.
The sun slips, the skyline a slope of dove-pink ice and here, even stars cannot stand.
The air, sweet as rum, swallows the sundered sun. It is squeezed dry and
pomegranate juice wells against the crystal horizon and the after-shocks of
light spill into the darkling valleys as mist. The porch bubbles with laughter and life.
He plays the guitar, as golden-brown as the flowing ale, for the musical mountains.
And they listen. Then the stars. Diamond troves of space.
Splinters of ice catching low light. Dark falls.

MARCH 21 9:17 AM

The scales are tipping and the lord of spring, at the tug of
ancient melodies braided through the world by secret fires and old tales,
has begun to banish the hounds of winter. The white wick is guttering

out and at last a green flame, woven of leaves and flowers and sun,
has caught and enveloped the holy candle of seasons.

MARCH 22 10:00 PM

As I wander these strange, familiar streets, I see
the ghosts of the past swim before me like pearlescent shapes in
the dusk of memory. And yet, I can see a golden thread, a strand
of luminous silver running like a song amid all my years
and sojourns. The silver of your grace and the song of your love.

MARCH 23 8:00 AM

I opened my eyes this cloudy spring morning and woke to a
welling of trills and soft warbles—a net of birdsong branching the air
in liquid notes and golden tones that seemed to utter more than all I've
ever said. I realized that if the Maker can draw praise from these, the
frailest of creatures, then how much more should I be willing to sing!

MARCH 24 10:27 PM

These last few nights, my face has hurt for so much laughter.
My cheeks bunch like red apples then recline back into smooth hillsides
beneath two eyes glowing like evergreen pools, and I find in this ache,
this bright and gladsome sorrow, longings for that city yet to come,
when all of the wrongs, the grievances and disasters,
are subsumed into the peal of the King's wild laughter.

MARCH 25 11:08 PM

Goodbyes. I dread their coming, yet accept their prevalence over
a life drenched with grief. Just as hard to handle as the first time they perched
like hawks against the pale horizon. I pace alone, late at night, in the
house, yearning for that day in which goodbyes are no longer a fragment of pain
wedged in history, when all I hold most dear shall sing and laugh beneath the vine,
and where belonging shall hush from every singing leaf, filling
every disembodied body with hope and every hopeless hope with final fulfillment.

MARCH 26 10:46 AM

To wander through this ragged soul would seem to uncover a wound
just opened, weeping a deluge of sorrow into this heart of mine.
It's a sorrow for things passing and an aching hope for what is yet to come.
Here in these shadowlands, grief is the currency by which we create,
yet longing is the eternal language by which we shall lift the veil from creation.

MARCH 27 12:26 PM

Birdsong through our doorway comes like a shimmering envoy refracting
from that thunderous song imbuing the very bones of creation.
Two birds in a winter wreath build a nest in which to practice the liturgy
of new life. The mother watches me now from the bald head of the

pear tree, a soft melody spilling from her throat like pools of liquid honey.

MARCH 28 10:21 AM

My heart is smitten and shattered, oh Lord, by the news of another school shooting: the young lives extinguished, the families fractured, the
constellations of community splintered by a storm of bullets.
How long, oh Lord? How long until our groaning ceases? Come, Lord Christ,
and heal all that is broken. Come, Lord King, and make us new!

MARCH 29 10:18 AM

How can it be that the world is so broken and yet so beautiful?
There may be darkness, but this morning it seems altogether drowned out
by running rivulets of light. I see you on the words in the page before me, in
the little chestnut-feathered birds on the feeder not ten feet away. I see you
in the snow glazing the grass and the music wrenching my heart into a
knot of wonder. You are in all things, Lord—teach me to see it, teach me to know you.

MARCH 30 10:14 AM

I think one day I'll write a tale about a vintage wine,
the wine of communion and crucifix blood poured out

on these grapes and vines. The wine that leavens creation and
makes each tree an oaken chapel, the wine that turned to death
when our First Mother ate that apple. And when thus my time draws near,
and my life is swallowed up, then I pray my Maker will help me bear that old, communion cup.

MARCH 31 6:03 PM

Spring has burst about this berth, making of creation
a breathing, lavish bower. Springtide carols flow in pearl
notes from the breasts of returning flocks and the trees are mint-green
with patches of moss. The air is heavy with the scent of rain
and new birth begins to stir at last upon these brown, resting hills.

IV

April

APRIL 1 4:53 PM

Strong wind was exhaled from the bowl of the lake today,
and now it rakes the treetops with a howl rising from deep wilderlands.
Bending branches, cracking timber: it's as if the trees speak to one another
in this roving tempest, perhaps telling the stories etched by long ages into their
bark, or dancing reels contained in their green rings, or perhaps still
yearning simply again to walk beneath the flaxen, springtide moon.

APRIL 2 9:53 AM

As one chapter of my life reaches its end, I look on this
next adventure as through a veil of mist: uncertain, shrouded.
I know not where this path might lead. And yet, I read today a prayer of
the Psalmist in which he exhorted me simply to trust, and if I can

manage that, then he will act. Therefore, my life is truly not my own. It is yours, my Maker, and yours alone.

APRIL 3 10:16 AM

When my body lies in ruin in the earth from whence I came,
will you gather the pieces like shattered glass, refashion, and make them new again?
And when you peel back this old creation, and those cloud-tossed meadows
I love are gone, when even the woodlands are swept with shadows and all I am left
with is what comes with the dawn, then can I be with you?
When you make it new, can I be with you—with you, my Lord?

APRIL 4 8:56 AM

Take me by the weary hand, cradle now this ragged heart.
For what lies ahead I fear I cannot face without your ever-abiding
presence draped like a cloak around me. Walk with me and guide me in the
shelter of your wings. Lead me into this hazy beyond with grace and goodness,
reminding me that I am first and always an emissary of your eternal Kingdom.

APRIL 5 12:36 PM

Last night, as we sped down the freeway, the night was sundered by glory. The wispy clouds were pasteled like Easter: powder blue

and mellow pink and soft, pale yellow—a pad of butter melting into the
burning sky. And when the colors faded and the stars winked on and on,
the moon, beacon-bright, beamed down on the earth,
and for but a moment, all in the world seemed right.

APRIL 6 10:36 PM

For the coolness of my love, the slackness of my zeal, and the
myriad ways I sacrifice daily upon the bloody altar of self,
I beseech your pardon, my King. These, after all,
like three rusty nails, held you to that blood-stricken tree
and betrayed you in the garden with a traitor's kiss. How can I thus
live when my sins stole your breath? Where is my hope—if there is any at all?
Where is my hope?

APRIL 7 9:48 AM

They took his body down from the tree with blood in its grooves.
The Word and Life lying lifeless on the ground.
The sky was dark—battered to a bruise and
his followers shrouded Him with linen and laid Him in a tomb.
His body broken and frail; the bride had murdered her Groom.

APRIL 8 9:52 AM

And in that tomb of dark and stone, the limning Word of God
did lay, and just as in the very beginning, he rested on the seventh day.

Six days of labor, but the seventh was the Lord's. The earth he made in time, but he rested when it was done. That tomb, then was like Eden,

and by His blood, Jesus blessed it. God rested.

APRIL 9 4:25 PM

Oh Christ, who conquered death and kneels now on its wretched throat, choking out its damnable life, may the light of your resurrection soak into the hardwood of my heart and into every atom of creation until it and I both burst forth with praise to the returning

King, the Lord of Lords, the Son of Man, who has opened a passage for

heaven to bleed back into this broken and beautiful world.

You have rent into shreds death's billowing shadow and even now it begins to fray. All praise is yours, Lord Christ, all loves, all hopes.

APRIL 10 8:52 AM

I wish I was holy. Holy like a song billowing on the wings of the dawn.

I wish I was holy. Holy and divine—filled to brimming with sweet, humble wine.

I wish I was holy. A priest set apart, but every green thing turns to rot in my heart.

I wish I was holy. But what can I do when everything within me steers away from you?

But you are the truth, you are the dawn, and you are the green that was there all along.

So soon, I'll be holy.

APRIL 11 10:07 AM

These streets, they are dusty and worn ragged with weary travelers who wander the way. The stones are so cold and these roads cracked and old and they seem to long for the day. But I'll climb up the watchtower, I'll go step by step, to the place at the top where I've sang and I've wept. I will climb up the tower to the sanctuary there. I will go to this Eden, go up stair by stair.

APRIL 12 10:32 AM

I look into the woods, standing at attention and shaded dark by this morning light. As the sun weaves golden through that patchwork of branches, I can see a refracted spray of color—as if through a prism of springtide—descend on these boughs. Each branch is painted with vestments of green, each dryad arrayed in gowns of emerald silk.

APRIL 13 10:35 AM

Birdsong: mellifluous and liquid, rising like pearls of water, like pools of melted stone from the throats of little birds. I sit and bask in the sound, the sound of singing that our King takes his pleasure in, the sound of praises welling from these frailest of things. So also, my God, draw praise forth from me!

APRIL 14 11:15 PM

Oh how furrowed and fell, how wild and waste is this heart inside my chest. It steeps with anger, with frustration and resentment:

some of it worthy in a sense, most unworthy. Such is my condition in this
fallen flesh. Yet Lord, through this anger, let me not devolve into a clanging
gate, allowing this boil I feel within to find harbor in something that takes
not into account your mercy, your grace, and your everlasting forbearance.
Not all anger is wicked, so this is a charged space in which I so desperately
need a Healer. Shape this heart then as you will and inject your
ever-present love into every atom of this which I am feeling tonight.

APRIL 15 11:19 PM

This room, I think, is a proper burrow of which a hobbit would approve,
with its faint scent of apple and cinnamon and oft turned pages, and
even the occasional smell of another world wafting through their words,
with the warm, yellow light falling like tawny leaves on the clock and various maps,
but most of all it is the desk, where new stories are spun and tales are told.

APRIL 16 5:00 PM

All here is waking from winter's cold thrall. The trees are wrapped now
in subtle leaves, as though they are remembering what it means to be green.

The trees strain and swell by piling rings in their bones
to pull golden life from the cloudy founts above and drink deeply of
the sunken pools below. All here is waking unto springtime's com-
ing Sabbath.

APRIL 17 5:56 PM

Sitting on the tree swing with the sound of birds and wind
flowing around me, I feel that creation is speaking or else striving for
utterance—preaching in words deeper than all I've ever said.
Away above me, the clouds clash and plume against the far horizon
in distant water, forming wind-blown shapes in the sky like fairy
ships.

APRIL 18 10:50 AM

A deep-chested blackbird, with red along its wings, wails aloud
a warning as I step out to the lawn. A triad of rusty-breasted
robins burst from their perches near the growling screen door.
There's a sparrow in the thickets and a finch standing sentinel on
the shed.
There's a bird in every treetop, each a soaring snatch of red.

APRIL 19 9:28 PM

Bolts of shattered light are hurled down from the heights
as if from the fists of mighty titans to this furrowed planet below
their
cloud-swelling thrones. And I think that for all the fury brewing in
those darkling

skies, when set beside the reckless, raging grace of the one who kindled those lights,
this storm may be called Tame or Still that fractures this rainy night.

APRIL 20 3:07 PM

My heart is filled to bursting with stories. They flow from my lips,
from my pen, from my eyes. And so full is this chest that it aches like
a lonely pang, a pang for a world I remember yet barely,
a pang that flares as a hot coal when the fire prong of story
stirs the embers again. It's a pang tended by tales, nurtured by stories, branded by songs.

APRIL 21 9:50 AM

From the cloud-tossed heavens brimming with dew,
to the storm-purple mountains stern-faced and noble;
from the cathedral-columned forests putting forth new leaves,
to the sapphire sea leaping endlessly with light and foam,
all creation yearns in groaning symphony for the new Jerusalem to descend.

APRIL 22 4:42 PM

I lie on my stomach in this cold spring air and study the tree
that reposes beside me. Its weathered, knobby, dragon-scale feet
are planted firmly in the earth and I imagine that they must soar down
and down forever into vast caverns and worlds unseen. It's two-limbed

body of limber brown and mossy green, lifts high above me like a banner
spread to full furl on the wind. And above my head, a canopy of young,
rust-orange leaves trembles against a slate gray sky.

APRIL 23 5:55 PM

The pear tree outside has clothed herself in a wedding gown of
swirling, linen-pure white. The strands of her long, liquid hair are
stirred and combed by the cold breeze—as fresh and as bright as
a sun-tossed sea. The birds in her boughs, each one a little bridesmaid,
prepare their leaf-laden sister to walk fully into spring and wed herself at
last to the great, laughing lord she finds waiting there.

APRIL 24 10:17 AM

I stand isolated on the edge of a vast promontory,
myself a little, quiet spider weaving yards of glowing, gossamer
thread from within myself—always musing, yearning, weeping, throwing,
searching these measureless oceans of mist for a place in which
these threads, these filaments, might one day catch.

APRIL 25 10:20 AM

The smell of green, of growing things, waltzes like a breath
of light on the breeze. These ever-weary roads are fringed anew
by pastels of pink and red and orange and gold and white.

Whispers of green in the cracks of pavement. Rumors of life
in these broken stones. Seeds and stories even in the shattered.

APRIL 26 2:29 PM

Your promises, oh God, seem to drip with truth when all around
me is sun and peace and laughter. But when the world wends downward
as the world bends now—when I am tired and anxious, when my plans
have gone awry—how will I choose to respond? Will you grant me the courage
to still believe your promises are true even when life does not go my way?

APRIL 27 10:32 AM

Is the lord of spring not a jolly, red-apple cheeked artist
whose laughter rolls from deep in his hearty chest and frolics merrily
along the waking earth? In each of his footfalls, green bursts from the ground.
When his eyes rove the wood, his brother star spills golden wine. In each towering laugh,
in every thunderous song, this lord of spring casts his brush o'er the
world and summons an enchantment of color from winter's gray canvas.

APRIL 28 5:20 PM

What is wind? Is it the result of atmosphere and shifting systems
of irresistible, natural course? Is it the movement of air as the world

hurtles through the diamond troves of space? Is it breath gusting from the lips of
monsters or snoring old men? Or is it yet that still, steady *ruakh* exhaled
from the chest of the limning Maker, the incarnate Word that is, even now,
hovering over the wild deep to draw a suffusion of song from the swirling chaos?

APRIL 29 9:13 AM

Light has dawned through these window panes like golden spears splintering a film of ice, and I rise from my bed and throw wide the curtains and gaze with wonder at the waking world. The bowl of night brimmed over with the sweet draught of sleep and the left hand of dawn cradles my fading dreams.

APRIL 30 5:20 PM

The sky spans endless along this acre-bridging freeway like a vast sea marked by faint, white pen strokes on an old, yellow-hide map. It flows beyond these stubbled fields laden with waves of dewy moss and I begin to wonder in this hopelessly poetic soul where the blue sky-waters end and where the many waters of space begin.

V

May

MAY 1 9:19 AM

Wind combs the garland of branches overhead,
shaking droplets of rain free from these young, waking leaves.
I can't help but wonder if a ghost—a Ghost, mind you—stirs them.
Word yet unspoken, benevolent yet unseen—unseen not because this Ghost
is less real, but because he is so infinitely real that we cannot
perceive him. In the end, perhaps it is we who are the ghosts.

MAY 2 3:02 PM

These daily poems, these songs from the stillness, are
each moment, in themselves, a solitary battle. For I lament again how
backward silence is in this world's economy. To linger and prayerfully watch
creation speed ever toward a coming redemption is all the object of my yearning.
Be still. It's so simple, yet not even this can I fully obey.

MAY 3 4:28 PM

Young leaves shaking in this crisp, dew-spring breeze.
Emerald turf speckled with swaying veins of shadow.
A yellow roof of branches above this arboreal court. Great wisps
of cloud like a naiad's stream-foam hair. I sit on the swing and
my heart wells with praise in this growing, green hall.

MAY 4 8:58 PM

The space between the sun's rest and the rising of the stars,
when the birds begin to roost in the dewy clefts of trees,
when the sky is pink as powder and the clouds as blue as mountains
at dusk, when light yet fills the bowl of night and every leaf lies still,
in this magic hour, this afterglow, I sense a solemn whisper:
a shadow foreshadowing the day when shadows lift and stillness at last begins.

MAY 5 12:00 PM

The flowers are opening and the lawn is speckled with a sprinkle of
coins. Dandelions spread yellow manes to catch the grinning sun.
In the front: a garden box of tulips—red and white—sway in sanguine
breeze, festooned by strands of purple-blue potted perennials.
Each little flower, like dewdrops of poetry gushing from the liquid lips
of the waters above and below, pronounces a love and magic divine,
The same love and magic that pronounced the flower of creation to unfurl long ago.

MAY 6 8:23 AM

The greening trees embroider the earth as with shimmering thread and I stand on the porch as the sun tumbles away into the bowl of dusk, lost in the folds of time and space. Even I forget who I am, where I come from and where I am destined to go, because for this one moment, I am already there, already swept up in the great dance restored, made new, made right.

MAY 7 7:43 PM

I hope to lay out on the lawn this night and gaze out into realms of starlight: those globes of pearlescent poetry gleaming down upon these young, yellow-veined leaves. Perhaps I'll try to count their icy myriads, to number their glimmering hordes, and think of my father Abraham
and how one of those stars had been lit for me.

MAY 8 9:39 PM

The Lord is my Shepherd, the Good Shepherd who watches o'er his flock. I am led gently through green meadows and I drink from cold, running streams. Yet yawning ever before me like a black maw bristling with fangs, is a dark shadow and I tremble for fear of what
awaits me in that hellish place. But the Shepherd with the song from his lips
and the staff in his hand pierces the heart of the valley of the shadow of
death by passing through it before me.

MAY 9 9:28 AM

Here in this chapel of creation, as dawn shatters the
black stone of night, I seek you again, oh King of earth and heaven.
Lead me by your mercies this day, that all upon which I embark
might fit firmly within the ever-spun tale of your will. Keep me from
temptation, Father, and let me live in each holy moment
as an heir and an emissary of your eternal Kingdom.

MAY 10 10:17 AM

The droning of the highway rolls ever on like a chorus of machines
vomiting fumes that rise as deadly toxins and swell upon the breeze,
slowly desecrating this world upon which our Maker has borne his fingerprints.
And yet, I hear also the songs of sparrows and see a robin alighting within
her palace and smell the green scent of growing things. Beauty is here
among the darkness, and this beauty—fragile and sweet—erupts
yet from the wreckage of broken.

MAY 11 2:40 PM

A bird on the feeder, framed by wind-stirred leaves, reaches its little
head in then out again, flapping for balance with delicate, brown wings.
It is kept by peace and the least suspicion of who truly put those
seeds there in the first place. It feeds, then flies away with a carefree song.
Am I not also like one of these? A small, altogether silly creature,

so frail, yet so beloved, feeding unawares from a hand I never
choose to see.

MAY 12 8:32 AM

All is still and sacred as here, the dawn, like a glowing coal,
flares red and golden in the east, beset by many winds.
All is wild and wonderful as each leaf, like an emerald ember,
shakes and spins and rustles and quakes the language of trees.
All is grand and glorious; all is song and still.
My eyes are filled with wonder, my whole life long they will.

MAY 13 10:31 AM

The Mighty One, the Lord, the Maker, the Word
speaks and summons the earth from the rising of the sun
to its sinking down. Each moment within moments, each passing
web of trickling seconds written and penned by His Majesty's quill,
etched in the fabrics of time and history, a limning poem limning
all into being.

MAY 14 4:35 PM

How green is the green against the gray, the gray slate of cloud,
and how soft is the soft of swaying leaves, and the leaves of grass on this
garden ground. The silver of the pools reflects the sky as though in the
gaze of a crystal well and the wind-rush runs o'er the ruffled
river like the twinkling hush of a tolling church bell.

MAY 15 4:40 PM

As I gaze at the blue between clouds, my soul catches again that song at which even clouds must pause in their passing,
and the hills must break forth in praise; at which the cold mists dance and the willows
softly weep and the rivers, like running twine, search, search, searching for that language
that only it can know, that lost tongue that renders naiads again and bids all creation wake.
Creation waits for us, it yearns for us, to speak once more that ancient Song and sing again that olden speech.

MAY 16 8:59 AM

Shadows of leaves fall to the ground, refracted by the green boughs above. They move in much the same way—rustling and chattering against their wind-blown brothers, and yet they are only a shadow. But perhaps even the branches too are mere shadow themselves, refracted by the Trees that stand rooted in the fabrics of time,
the great Trees in that far country that we one day will dance beneath.

MAY 17 9:04 AM

Oh Lord, I have at last completed that which I labored four years to write!
A first novel, a rite of passage, a hidden door to a secret garden upon which every
author must knock. I am met now with an intoxicating rush of joy and hope

and longing and sorrow, yet these feelings are naught if not anchored
first in you. I give you this novel, this compilation of fractured words put into splintered
sentences and composed into a feeble story. May your Spirit breathe into these pages
that they might ruffle with the scent and sound of your Kingdom coming
to earth. Use even this work of battered creation to advance the tale you
proclaim o'er your world. Guide me now from here, my Maker,
into all you have written down in your own deep Chronicles.

MAY 18 3:51 PM

We began to prepare the garden: soil turned and tilled to receive
green roots and bountiful fruit, tended by drenching sun and falling rain.
The peach trees are garmented with leaves, the rose bushes yet half-bare, the
raspberry and blackberry put out white star flowers above thorny stalks.

MAY 19 5:18 PM

A small tree, scarcely a sapling to these shadowing, leafy giants,
casts its five-limbed figure o'er the sun-sprayed earth.
Lithe and limber, like an elvish maid dancing in the courts
of a wooded realm, it raises beads of fragrant hair to the blue heavens:
garlands of green, braids of brown, locks of dewy violet.

MAY 20 3:32 PM

I find myself in a kiln of fear, as the future looms like a ghoul, a specter before
my eyes. Yet I pray, great Architect of Light and Life, that you might teach
this weary soul how better to anchor my heart in the peace of your presence
that you might lift my head beyond this drain of days and reveal the grand scape
of eternity stretching forever between stars and boiling nebulae.
Help me treaty with my future and recall ever to mind who it is that shapes the path before me.

MAY 21 3:28 PM

Six days of labor spent that Sunday might find Sabbath,
a sanctuary of respite among these boiling, bustling mills of life.
Yet still they heave and cough and belch black smog, obscuring
the blue air and green meadows from whence these poems flow.
How hard to find rest in a world so strained and frantic!
How hard to find rest, oh Christ, in any but you!

MAY 22 9:16 PM

The moon hangs o'er the blushing west: a silent sickle of ice
festooned by faintest brush-strokes of purple clouds.
Birds trill sleepily in anthem from leafy bowers and
whisper dreamy secrets in the maple's tangled, arboreal ear.
And if I listen closely, I can hear this night unfold
like the sound of pages turning, or candles flickering away.

MAY 23 4:01 PM

Each breath of passing breeze seems to gust from the Maker's lips,
hushing like a phantom through these wishing shadowlands.
Each slow exhalation—cool and fresh, stirring the boughs
of high trees, pulling at the rope swing—bears fragrances
of wandering petals. A roving rumor of a love both human and divine.

MAY 24 1:24 PM

A tune spun by the turning of the world, that has rolled ever on since its melodious birth:
mercies are new! Behold, all things are new! God's mercy in the morning beams
out across the earth, through frost on the windowpanes and dew on the grass.
Mercy, saluting the old way of yesterday and heralding the newness streaming from the dawn.
Mercy, speeding always west and west: to the sea, the peaks, the hills, then back, back again.

MAY 25 10:39 PM

To sit and breathe silence is a sacrament I too often neglect,
yet on this night, stillness comes simply. As garlands of lights illumine
standing rows of books like sentries or columns of trees spanning the
green wood, as the air lilts softly with the scents of apples and bakeries

and cinnamon, as the clock keeps beating out the steady unfolding
of time, all is as it should be and for now, the world is at peace.

MAY 26 10:36 AM

The wood is a standing lullaby. Silent pines assemble in the gathering
dusk and the westering sun flakes through as willow-wisp fine as candy floss
to rest golden upon beds of moss. We pass among the pines amid
frothing manes of water that melody the air with mist. We whisper past the trees
like phantoms to the wood, roaming the borderlands of mountain and
airless orbit. I feel as if I could scratch the sky's underbelly.

MAY 27 6:50 PM

The song of the deep when the sea is calm and it laps against the shore
ripples and rolls like a hymn of water, like a luminous strain of lore.
But the song of the deep when the sea is feathered by waves and thunder and foam,
echoes and grumbles like a billowing behemoth and through sunken caverns it roams.
Two songs of the deep by the Maker composed, two songs of the deep as one.
Two songs of the deep—a pale ringlet of rose—like fire until history is done.

MAY 28 10:08 AM

What is grace? It is a swirling, raging array of wisping color, of foaming
Water, a melody and poem, a fairy tale that has invaded the bones
of reality and shaken the very roots of myth and fact.
What is grace? It is the source and object of all we endeavor to create.
It is the sun, the cloudless sky, the golden trees: grace is in all things.

MAY 29 5:28 PM

One wisp of cloud o'er the treetops; one swath of foam
on a calm, blue sea, one thread of cotton abandoned on a
tablecloth, one snowflake of wool forgotten by the loom,
one downy, little feather floating upon a forest stream,
one pale rumor of mist pooling in a wooded vale.

MAY 30 4:32 PM

The night sky is spangled with stars o'er these rolling hills
of wheat churning like amber waves across the flatlands.
And yet there's sickness in the air and poison in the wells
and many griefs that plague the unfolding years and spill tears on every face.
You are my country, but never my home, oh land of my sojourn.

MAY 31 10:18 AM

Refocus my eyes, aim my compass, grant me strength to
stumble along as best as I can this path you've placed before my feet.

Hold me fast as I walk and weep. Clutch me tighter to your wild love
even as I clutch after fleeting shadows. Guide me through this veiled land
and unto the hills of New Eden, and if I bleed on the road, let it be to your praise.

VI

June

JUNE 1 11:19 AM

A night past, I was driving through the country as the golden hour
billowed like song in the west—chords of crimson, melodies of moon,
percussion of pink, all rolling over the green pastures filled with wind.
My heart swelled with wonder as, for but a moment,
two divorced worlds converged again and seemed to become one.

JUNE 2 9:22 AM

The clearing outside rests in song and shade,
forged of old light handed down from leaf and bud,
filtered like golden droplets away into the heart of the
wood, a heart beating bursting green. The clearing rests
in shade and song, old light freshened by young, dewy leaves.

JUNE 3 7:00 PM

And if you read these songs, these spaces of stillness, I hope
you hear the forests stirring, I pray you feel the ocean crashing
on the cliffs of the Scottish Isles. I wish I could
be there to see them, nine years past I was, and
I feel the weight of love here now as I did once then.

JUNE 4 7:08 PM

A bald eagle roosts in a lonely pine on the sinews of this cliffside.
Along the spanning deep they roll, unfolding like
faces, like rings in a tree, and round every bend, a new
range of cliffs, piling ever outward like the mountains
of Aslan's Country in which every range is greater than the last.

JUNE 5 5:22 AM

I cannot know, oh Lord, every reason why sleep so evades me.
Perhaps it is this racing of mind, or maybe yet the discomfort
of body, or perhaps it is something other altogether. Whatever it may be,
I would not scorn even this time of un-sought-after wakefulness, for what
great mysteries might you be preparing to reveal even now in this restless night?

JUNE 6 9:19 PM

In spite of all this wrong, in spite of all the pain,
in spite of the bombed-out villages and homeless orphans

and those shunned by society, there is yet much that goes right
and beauty brims through creation like a warm drink on a winter's night.
For though the Kingdom is for now but a whisper and a shadow,
it descends ever nearer, like a song in the clouds.

JUNE 7 4:13 PM

Many years have faded now behind a landscape of fading memory
and here on the cusp of the life ahead, I take a deep draught of stillness.
Thou hast carried me through garden and storm,
through storm and garden I have passed.
Now one thing I ask thee, my Shepherd and King,
that these next numbered years might be fuller than the last.

JUNE 8 9:19 AM

If this world is, as the poets say, soaked with mystery and riven with magic,
then what if a puddle were really a portal to a mirror-realm
of waters and falling dew? What if a cluster of stones reflect high mountains
beyond the walls of time? What if golden sunlight plunging
through branches like flaxen tassels opens breaches
in the fabrics of creation where joy might one day brim and overflow?

JUNE 9 9:10 PM

Birdsong spills from trembling leaves, like a promise that one day
these trees will rise anew to sing and laugh and roam the
deep woods under a starry dome. Rosy cider is brewed in the
west and it runs over the bowl of night, surging
o'er the horizon's thread as by the breaking of a dike.
And in its blushing luster, the trees are colored like a robin's breast.

JUNE 10 9:20 AM

I sit behind the screen door with a sigh as the morning clouds
waft lazily through the powder-blue sky. My heart, I find, is drawn
down a thousand avenues, yet as the minutes flow around me
and the rabbits bound through dewy grass and cardinals soar over the
shoulder of hedges blooming white, I find a peace, a peace light and
pure as if these clouds were pages turning over the storybook of creation.

JUNE 11 10:12 PM

I once thought that poems were contained in dewdrops falling from willows
and beaded by fairies on the grass. I thought that they guttered and died
like a candle weary of burning in the mundane rush of homework and groceries
and computers and vehicles trundling across the highway. Where is the art in this?
I wondered. But I have since learned that poems are everywhere: in stones swept onward

by the surf, in cracked sidewalks littered with broken liquor bottles,
in autumn trees shuddering in the crackle-crisp air, in the
haggard, worn-out visages of heaven's ragged priesthood. All things
carry poems if we give them the decency of looking and molding
them into something new.

JUNE 12 10:59 AM

If our Lord uses the fractured and fissured soul
to further his encroaching Kingdom, then I consider the other inadequate
things, the blights we overlook and scarcely notice as we rush along our way.
Could eternal destinies be written in crumpled leaves or broken twigs?
Could mountains and forests and hills hold somehow the keys to history and hope?

JUNE 13 11:54 AM

"This is Christ's body, broken for you." These words are uttered in the sacred
hush of frosted glass, among gathered saints with diamond eyes
gleaming out the morning light, in the glow of all these little temples
filling the wooden pews. Christ's body broken, the Maker unmade.
Broken like this world with its wars and tears, broken like this shattered
clergy taking counsel with the King here among sacrament and saint,
broken that by breaking, all brokenness might at last be unmade.

JUNE 14 9:40 AM

I sit in the morning silence, birdsong passing from air to air,
clock marking, moment by moment, the steady unfurling of time.
I sit and whisper feeble prayers under my breath. So unworthy:
I, a small, sniveling creature, formed of soil and grime,
communing with the Maker who spun galaxies as stories and composed
rivers as songs. Yet as I whisper in this stillness, I feel as if a multitude
of saints gathers around me—stained glass drenched with sunlight, choirs
dripping honey voices, ancient pews soaking in the dulcet sound,
and all of a sudden, I know that the Maker is here with me, and the ordinary becomes holy.

JUNE 15 10:34 AM THE GHOST I

Look, look
out over the stars wheeling in the reaches
of dusty moons lending their luminescence to the ebbing whisper.
Watch the tremulous glow murmur
as the Ghost who yet haunts the star-brimming oblivion
wavers and whistles through the shapeless expanse
like a wandering, winnowing wind as it orchestrates
birdsong and beads dew and paints the horizon aflame.
Look, look
and see that for every encroaching inch of broken,
there remains still a slight, silent remnant of beauty.
For a Ghost haunts the ground that we tread and rustles like a
dream unseen to the eye, but look long enough and you will see.

JUNE 16 11:06 AM THE GHOST II

Listen, listen
to the haunting strain that rises like vapor and billows like a valley mist,
that spills out even from the fragments of nature, listen as it delves
and dips—ethereal yet known, otherworldly yet familiar—for the Ghost
draws forth his melodies from the very splinters of our inadequacy.
Listen to song welling—an echo of its soon-to-come glory—in your bones and
Listen, listen
as it flows too in resonance from the earth-emboweled fibers
of the very ground beneath the searching dusk.
And one day the Ghost will emblazon the burrowing black,
but for now there's a distant song beyond the draping silence.
Listen long enough and you will hear.

JUNE 17 11:13 AM THE GHOST III

So earnestly look and fervently listen
for we are restless bards of a far-off Kingdom,
homesick for a home we've never had and
aching and breaking both for a land near at hand
yet again so distant. But listen, look, pay attention to the moments
you weep without a reason, for it could be that the Breathing Breath, the
Benevolent Ghost is breathing his breath into your deepest hopes.
So watch for the Ghost and rest in this haunting.

JUNE 18 5:02 PM

Unshackle your attention if only for a moment. Your eyes yearn
to wander the never-ending scape of sky piling like liquid shelves up and up,
even into the diamond troves of space. Your free-roaming heart pines to soar beyond
these waves of information and machine to delve further up and deeper in
until the smoke-embroiled clang of automation fades at last into everlasting stillness.

JUNE 19 8:54 AM OUT THE WINDOW I

I'm looking out the window this morning, the curtains ruffling like
swan wings. Unseen crickets chorus in anthem from beneath the windowsill
as fireflies douse their lamps, surrendering to dawn. Beads of
dew, strewn by fairies, hang like Christmas ornaments, like
dwarven earths from stalks of grass, sheathing swords against
pattering squirrel feet: fluid baubles on soft blades.
Godfather trees stoop curiously over the sloping lawn, sending envoys
of twigs, leafy ambassadors, to counsel with the ground—rumors
of the doings of Mr. Robin or Mrs. Owl, of the view
from above, or that from below—these councils of summer.

JUNE 20 9:17 AM OUT THE WINDOW II

Unicorns peer out from the shadowed wood, horns alive in flowing color.
Dragons are birthed from the clouds, rainbows of lights pouring

from plated scales like waterfalls. From the thickets: elves, flaxen hair falling
beneath silver helms, arrows springing lithely from supple rosewood.
Fairy tales incarnate. I'm looking out the window at a
wakening, brightening world, seeing myths dance in sunburst showers,
spying on the wandering roam of Ents, eavesdropping on the mumblings
of trees, because I have chosen to see more than there is.
The secret? There is always more than there is when
I touch pen to paper while looking out the window.

JUNE 21 6:36 PM

I have, oh Lord, been entrusted with the sacred story of another:
a pearl emblazoned as with falling sunlight, maimed perhaps by a
lifelong sorrow, yet shimmering still with echoes of beauty. Let me,
great Storyteller, guard this tale, this canticle of grief for the
one who bestowed it upon me. Lord, I know not what wonder you wait to
weave from her horror, but I pray in this meantime that you might anoint her in peace.

JUNE 22 12:54 PM

When music nets the air in bright, mellifluous pattern,
a fragment of Eden-fyre wedged like an ember within my soul
stirs and begins to burn. Burning for joys I have yet to sing, burning
in lament for a world burdened yet with all the aches and ills of this
present exile, burning to at last take flight and soar o'er eternity's flowing shoulder.

JUNE 23 9:58 AM

They came again last night: those voices oozing foul streams
into this sanctuary. Doubts about the future: have my paths
truly been laid in pleasant places? Doubts: doubts about—if you
boiled it down—the goodness of the King. So come close
to me, oh Christ. Breathe upon me, oh Spirit. Lead me on, oh Father.

JUNE 24 10:19 AM

I take note of a simple wonder this morning. The sight of a
red-breasted robin framed by green leaves that stir ever
gently the summer's mild breath. It perches with little feet
on a sweeping pencil stroke, pulling at a length of twine
caught in the tree. After a minute of tugging and madly flapping
wings, the robin lifts off from the branch and flies away.

JUNE 25 10:46 PM

I close my eyes with my feet in the cool, wet grass and listen,
simply listen to the wind raking the darkling treetops.
They murmur like water against a low, mossy bank. Beside me, the
buzz of the freeway is trundled by glowing spheres of speeding
yellow,
and above me, the sound of my father preparing our home for rest.

JUNE 26 6:49 PM

Sabbath descends, a cleft in time, and I hide myself here
that the glory of the Most High might pass me by.
As I rest in a stillness showered down from these hills,

I hear again that deeper tone bleeding from my very bones:
the ancient resonance of a song that shaped the world.

JUNE 27 10:48 AM

What if beneath the gilded moon, the trees roam the woods?
What if streams and forest pools brim with water spirits?
What if the poet has peeled back the veil with a whetted pen,
and seen beyond into a thing more real than dead waters and frozen trees?
What if the legends and tales are true? for myth in Christ has met and fused.

JUNE 28 9:50 PM

This little tree is like a little chapel: leaves rustling like praising
parishioners, boughs branching like pillars, like steeples to uphold the
doming roof, capsules hanging like stained glass, like fresh life,
reminding me of those who went before and of all the glory still to
come, rooted to the earth for the health of the ground,
reaching to the skies for the wonder of the clouds,
ever watchful, ever waiting to shed leaf and load, to
put on new form and be wedded like a bride.

JUNE 29 10:56 PM

So many, I've noticed, are afraid of the night. They search beneath
beds for monsters of their own fancy as fears assail with dripping fangs.
I wonder why this is, for as I stand outside at the laying to rest

of this passing day, I am struck with the beauty of the darkness that is
yet somehow bright with mother moon and her horde of starry sons
mapping out the form of constellations as they have done for centuries.
I can't help but think that, at its core, we are afraid of the dark because it
is still and stillness invites contemplation and contemplation allows us
to see ourselves as we truly are.

JUNE 30 10:31 PM

I sat on the beach today and watched in awe as the setting of the sun
seemed to turn and twist as if swept along by a billow of wind-writhing snow
to form above the water a three-pronged crown
of orange that melted gradually into pink. And I remembered in a rush
the King who wears that vast, cloudy corona upon his laughing brow
and of His banner and seal that emblazon this groaning world over.

VII

July

JULY 1 2:09 PM

A spectral shroud hangs o'er the lake like the tattered sails of a ghost ship wrecked and sundered along the foaming shore. The edge of its ragged cowl is a dyke of pouring mist raised against the still water. Imposing and tall, it stands sentinel over the cold, summer deeps.

JULY 2 9:35 PM

A heartglow of golden embers glows on a wide hearth and spills mellow like flowers and honey from the skyline to the earth. A young rabbit watches, cotton ball tail like a globe of snow furling above the freshly cut grass, its velvet nose twitching as clouds of fireflies billow by.

JULY 3 10:54 PM

What if fantasy were history and myth were fact?
What if there was a vast, eternal sea of living waters,
waters that contained every world ever created, and what if
those worlds held fauns and satyrs and centaurs and the rest?
What if every tree on our earth was like a doorway that bears
ancient tales as it drinks from sunken pools still pregnant with
droplets sired by that swirling sea? What if, within each of us,
a diamond of that same water was planted by the World Maker,
that even in forgetting we may remember and even in wasting we
may ever yearn?

JULY 4 10:32 PM

I bid thee pardon, oh Maker and King, for my thoughts are too small
and too few. Scarcely have I truly considered how your Kingdom
and country advance out into the myriad reaches of creation.
You are the Wolf King, the Lord of Lilies, the Maker of Mountains.
You are the Lord of Scotland, the King of Nigeria, the Prince of
Paraguay.
You are the King of Home, the Horse Lord, the Emperor of Galaxies.
You are the Lord of Green Valleys and the Spinner of Stories.
You are Christ the Messiah, Firstborn of womb and
grave, oh Christ the Lord, King of everything.

JULY 5 11:05 AM

Bless this new adventure that lies now before me,
for without your divine appointment resting upon it,
I cannot hope to succeed. Guide me by your mercy,

fill me with your peace, sanctify me by your Spirit, so
that I may, in all things, wear your name well, oh Christ.

JULY 6 8:54 PM

You are here, yes even here, even now, oh great Weaver of Life.
You are in the green of the trees, in the soft breeze that
stirs them, in the golden light suffused by the setting sun,
in the faces gathered like burnished constellations
around me. May you also dwell in this poem I write.

JULY 7 9:16 PM

For every flavor—for the sweetness of berries harvested
from the garden, for the sunny taste of tomatoes bursting
with seeds, for the savor of yeast rising from bread,
for the soft, mellow tang of cheese and almonds,
for every different flavor—I give thee thanks.

JULY 8 12:41 PM

As we begin this journey onward into the northern reaches of
this land—for a journey it is, not marked by swords or ancient
relics, but rather by time away and fellowship with those you
have given me to call family—I would be remiss if I did not beseech
your
tender mercy to abide in and around us as we go forth.
Be with us, guide us, walk alongside us.

JULY 9 7:58 PM

Spanning fields sprawl like bronzed seas from horizon
to mist-dimmed horizon. Waves of dusting pollen
waver in shafts of sunlight like motes of falling gold.
Spanning fields wander like maps beneath cloud-pearled skies,
filling this hour with golden hopes and golden prayers and golden dreams.

JULY 10 10:54 AM

Great shoulders of rugged stone line the roadway, clothed like fallen kings
in vestments of royal green and showered by pools of liquid gold.
The ground around them is ruddied and rusty with pine needles
shaken loose from the stand of evergreens that watch the waters
ripple by in raiments of waterweed and garlands of lilies.

JULY 11 10:37 AM

I delve into the mystery, I aim my compass further up and
further in: up and up, higher and higher, until dimension is riven through
with dimension, until Time itself begins all at once to work backward:
reversing, refining, restoring back to that Lost Garden
at the steady sigh of our Poet God, our Maker King.

JULY 12 4:22 PM

It may be true that I yearn for adventure in a deep chamber of my soul that is filled
with yellowed maps and faded cloaks, a traveler's staff in hand as I journey
from Shireland with a band of merry dwarves. And yet, yet when the
sun gets low and the trees are sprinkled with golden wine, I
begin to yearn with a vicious ache for something I can only call 'Home.'

JULY 13 5:13 PM ASLAN'S COUNTRY I

I long to breathe the air of my native land, to wander the forested hillsides
of my true country. I long to lie alone in the dusk and listen to the voice
that echoes with love and thunder, to feel the crisp unfolding of autumn
as it hushes through fields of waking heather and gently ruffles the
far stands of silver oak and starry willow. I long to climb a twilit rise
and watch as time changes the light into a symphony of falling color,
to sit in the fertile silence as the bracing wind wreathes the gilded
hollows in a veil of shimmering mist. Oh Lord, how long?

JULY 14 9:18 AM ASLAN'S COUNTRY II

I long to gaze into the piling ledges of space and marvel as
the fledgling pastels of a million, million points of light flicker
like lanterns in a frosty pane, to lie in the sweet grass
and feel the ground thrumming with the tenor of yawning

mountains and hear the breeze, swollen with windlore,
whisper through the assembling clover. Oh Lord, how long?

JULY 15 9:26 AM ASLAN'S COUNTRY III

I long to run through wooded pastures, to dance beside laughing springs,
to melt into wonder, to swim headlong up the sides of waterfalls
ringing still with the high, holy notes that bid her waters wake,
to stand in all the glory of the gloaming and close my eyes as
a song rustles by—ancient as the roots of the earth and new as the morning—
engulfing me with a great affection I could never hope
to earn or understand. Oh Lord, how long?

JULY 16 9:28 AM ASLAN'S COUNTRY IV

I long to gaze down into a valley alive with flecks of green and gold
and let the sight of wine-red vineyards and budding glades and
candlelit cottages inundate this storm-battered soul with sweet
belonging, to ramble across a wild countryside swathed
in blooming gardens and shaking hedges and burbling falls. Oh Lord, how long?

JULY 17 7:21 PM ASLAN'S COUNTRY V

I long to roam burgeoning hillsides in the faery glow of dawn and weep
in that quiet, sweeping gladness as the lily-white wood shivers
in the clutch of icy stars, to tremble in the throes of the

weight of glory as beams of gold rend apart the clouds to embrace a stand of
grandfather cedar and godfather pine. Oh Lord, how long?

JULY 18 7:27 PM ASLAN'S COUNTRY VI

I long to soar above the wind-swept plains and along the pillared
fringes of a fragrant orchard and listen to the gentle cadence of evening rain
dripping on leaves and limber boughs, to stroll the terraces of a bridge
draped with ivy and lean out over the wooden rail,
watching the river rush and froth and cascade along grassy banks. Oh Lord, how long?

JULY 19 4:20 PM ASLAN'S COUNTRY VII

I long to recline at the Table and take my seat among my beloved,
breaking bread, pouring wine, making merry beneath the vine,
to lay back my weary head and watch the stars kindle in
the heavens through a silvery needlework of branches and listen to the
songs sung, to the tales told, to the laughter shared. Oh Lord, how long?

JULY 20 5:26 PM ASLAN'S COUNTRY VIII

I long to enter through the doorway that I might be claimed as
a citizen of Estelar, a subject of Aslan's Country, a resident
of the Promised Land, to find that the holy homesickness within
me has been eternally quenched. I long to converse with

the Comforter, sow with the Savior, and plant with the Prince,
to see at last all things as they were meant to be, to travel further up
and further in forever and for all of time. Oh Lord, how long?

JULY 21 10:41 PM

The streets of Quebec City: roamed by vacant-eyed destitutes,
wreathed by pungent cigarette smoke, cobblestone avenues alive
with nightlife, taverns spilling music and laughter into the river-hazy
sky, the marble facade of palaces rising above sloping lawns.
The streets of Quebec City boil with a humanity who all in some measure
bear the mark of their Lord, Maker, Father, and King.

JULY 22 8:10 PM A LITURGY I

I am such an inadequate offering, oh Lord; I am but a small,
jagged, insignificant piece of clay. And I see that all the clearer
in this respite before the storm ensues, before I take up my pen as a
sword and toil a resistance that rails ever against any inkling of beauty.
Yet you, oh Christ, are the true source of beauty that glimmers with
every feeble heartbeat and you offer that which can never spoil nor fade.

JULY 23 8:14 PM A LITURGY II

After all, that very resistance sought to extinguish you once
and it failed. Yet now, even now, as my hand shakes with all its
frailty, this resistance strives to overcome me and rend apart this

passing creation. So gird me with your Spirit and craft a shield about
me that I might use my broken gifts, my fragmented abilities, to create that
which may reveal your beauty to a searching soul, something that might, in
your noble employ, be used to stir an honest longing for a new
country in which your beauty is manifested to all.

JULY 24 6:36 PM A LITURGY III

Use me to bless others, Lord; let me be as a tool in your hands,
because without you I am so weak, so insufficient, so prone
to wander into a love of the praise of people. Guard me,
Christ. Make me a man after your own heart, a man who deflects
any glory from myself and back unto the firstborn Author.

JULY 25 6:42 PM A LITURGY IV

Take control of this pen, my Lord, and let flow from it what you might
want to be read. May it please you by your Spirit to allow your beauty to
radiate out through this battered vessel, transfiguring it into a laughing
conduit of your blessing to others. I may be but a shattered pane, Lord,
a cracked and fractured flagon with nothing to offer this world. . .

JULY 26 4:11 PM A LITURGY V

. . .yet I am reminded of how you took the grotesque, the degenerate, the vile
and named them your saints. For where man failed on his own,
man is perfected in you. I am the very least of your servants,
oh Lord; I am a sniveling wretch with no plea, no reason to stake any claim.
I am so liable to lead others astray when left to my own devices.

JULY 27 4:13 PM A LITURGY VI

So reform me, renew me, let a river of new wine flow out
from me. May you billow through these incompetent words
and open long-cataracted eyes to the magic and mystery ever
around us. Help me to retreat and leave the stage to you
that your beauty may shine fully and unhindered
through that which I am endeavoring to write.

JULY 28 9:31 AM

I was at Niagara Falls the other day, watching the water
rise white in mist, then crash away o'er stone and shoal like
a stream of liquid glass. But even more lovely than these falls
were the people standing about me: every nation, every tongue,
every tribe and smell and color and hurt filling my vision with points of
life like a glimpse of when the Kingdom comes to earth.

JULY 29 10:01 AM

As summer reaches the fullest of its song, I marvel through the
window at this stained glass array of shades: roses unfolding yellow
and pink, the daffodils like golden stars, the blackberries are taking
on
vestments of faint purple, the garden beds are dusted with splashes
of red
and orange. All creation is a cathedral when we have eyes to see,
to see the wonder always and ever and all about.

JULY 30 11:18 AM

I was driving down 120th as morning birds sang from secret
perches and I watched the clouds shear apart like woolen
scrolls to admit a sudden plume of watery light to
fall around my car like celestial spears, gleaming on
wildflowers, drenching my soul for a moment in wonder.

JULY 31 10:33 AM

A breath, a stirring, a sudden flight, a lifting wing, a gust, an
upwelling, a snatch of melody, *ruakh*, a howling, a gale,
an exhalation, a draft, a phantom, an invisible power,
a force of pressure and temperature, an old man snoring in the
clouds, yet still I'm not sure what wind truly is.

VIII

August

AUGUST 1 6:14 PM

Oh great Bringer, Sustainer, and Author of Life, how I long to know what adventures you are writing me into, what unseen currents of narrative stir and shape me, how the characters around me align like constellations, pointing ever to the door of glory. You may, of course, never tell me this—you prefer to work in mystery—but with a twinkle in your eye you may stoop and say, "come and see."

AUGUST 2 9:28 AM

There are windows in the world, little chinks where something greater
glimmers through. Looking out *my* window, I see them in the suffusion
of wind-blown wildflowers, in the mushrooms parting the grass
like caps of ice, in leaves chattering greenly like breeze-stirred melodies.
There are windows here and everywhere: in molehills and

tree hollows and small, out-of-the-way puddles if only
first we look through the faithful eyes of a child.

AUGUST 3 6:39 PM

How I love when the weather turns cool—the air moving around me,
laden with memories of falling leaves and rainfall and childhood
laughter. Today, still in the drenching of summer, this little invasion
of autumn reminds me of all the joy yet to come
when the weather at last turns fall-crisp cold.

AUGUST 4 11:49 AM

I wonder today: does creation listen as we
live and laugh and scorn and sin? Does it marvel at our wisdom and
mourn for our foolery? Did our First Mother and Father know how
to speak with these watchful sentries of our affairs?
Could it be not that we cannot commune with creation
but that we have, perhaps, simply forgotten how?

AUGUST 5 8:30 PM

My eyes wander the sky from horizon to horizon as steadily as
an artist roving the landscape of a world ushered to being
on canvas. In the east, slates of white shattered by higher fields
of powdery blue. Above me, a pasture of cotton-bundles like the tails
of garden rabbits. In the west, the resting place of Mother Sun,
the clouds fizzle into golden heights and fringes of pink.

AUGUST 6 8:37 PM

Oh that all mankind might consider a rabbit and hearken as I do now
to the poem of simple existence it preaches from a pulpit of turf and
summer leaves. I watch as it sits still with ears twitching to listen to
the crickets chatter, huddled unafraid in this—its little domain in the wide
world. Its bead-black eyes are fixed on the skyline now fading to violet.
Still, ever peaceful, it glories and praises the Maker of Rabbits
in this temple wrought by a good, gracious King.

AUGUST 7 6:18 PM

There is poetry scrawled all through this world, stanzas of
buried grace contained in leaping crystals of water,
etched within the webbing of peach trees, hidden
away beneath the earth, secreted in branching roots.
Poetry is scrawled all through this world,
Rambling even through the halls of our hollow hearts.

AUGUST 8 10:18 PM

What is it that summons flame to the fragrant wick from
the void of shifting air molecules and the vast emptiness between atoms?
What is it that choreographs the dance of this little fire spirit
garbed in gowns of warmth and light? What is it about a candle flame
that so draws my eye? Is it the flickering unpredictability of moving
light? Is it the smell of Christmas or the memories of winter

days it resurrects within me? Or could it be because I recognize myself
within that flame? Here for a moment, then gone as the wick gets low.
Perhaps it will take my whole life long to give a name to the appeal of a candle.

AUGUST 9 5:36 PM

If all I did was watch the news, I think nearly all my hope
would burn, then simply melt away. To be sure, this world is wrecked and
tattered—temples of consumerism instead of Trees of Life—and man
is sundered too. But each day, as I walk into the coffee shop and
tie on my apron to serve Christ, I am filled to bursting with the wonder
that there is still good in this world. Man and woman, black and white,
adults and children, elderly and young—each seems riven with such joy,
with such generosity that I can't help but yearn for the day we'll all be new.

AUGUST 10 6:01 PM A LETTER FROM THE KING I

I am lovesick for you, my created ones. Do you not realize
the delirious longing I have for you? You were to be my faultless bride
and this world which you have sundered with unholy trysts and
foul communions was to be our wedding hall, our shared Kingdom!
But you have now built for yourself a shattered, mock kingdom in its stead;

AUGUST 11 6:28 PM A LETTER FROM THE KING II

A debased shanty-town in who's blind alleys the degraded gods
of greed and jealousy and hatred and envy and injustice of every stripe
and the warped spirits of a thousand, thousand tyrannies,
idolatries and adulteries gorge themselves on the ruins of a humanity
long spoiled. You have become hopelessly entangled by poisoned,
grasping brambles of your own design and in your despairing attempt to find
joy apart from your Groom, you have twisted yourselves into
monsters without plea or reason for salvation.

AUGUST 12 6:32 PM A LETTER FROM THE KING III

You illegitimate whores! You ragged harlots! For what has come
of that fruitless clutching after a pleasure that does not exist?
You have knotted families, shattered nations, corrupted histories,
wrecked your own innocence. I could have washed my hands of you long
ago. I could have justly poured out all the fury of my wrath upon the creation
you so happily desecrated! I could have abandoned you
in the brothels of your own rotting hearts!
But. . .

AUGUST 13 6:36 PM A LETTER FROM THE KING IV

. . .I am still lovesick for you, my created ones. So let me break
your heart that I might inhabit it. Let me unmoor all those things
untethered to myself. Let me bear your death. Let me reverse your

darkness and rend to pieces the shackles that hold you to this kingdom
of ruin. Let me tear out the choking weeds of poverty and disease and betrayal—

AUGUST 14 6:39 PM A LETTER FROM THE KING V

—that I may plant better cities and fresher gardens in their place.
Drown in my blood. Die in my death. Cast aside your paper crowns and
take up the wedding garland of my love for you. Let me heal the fractures
and splinters of a world long neglected by its caretakers. Let me bury all
rumors of violence, all whispers of conspiracy, all thrones of evil.
Let me love you. Let us—together—be wedded as we were once destined
that we might rule this new Kingdom I have in store as
Groom and bride, Creator and created, Lover and beloved.
For you are indeed beloved. You are precious. You are mine.

AUGUST 15 6:28 PM

It's easy to fear as the lightning strikes, like whips from the hand
of the Maker of Light. And sometimes it seems like he's causing
this fight as storms withdraw their blistering spikes. And the clouds
boil faster, faster still.
And the soil of my heart is furrowed and fell, and prayers are
like wishes, like coins in a well. I'm torn like the dirt and awaiting

the knell and wondering if you can harvest this shell, and the lightning
falls nearer, nearer still.

AUGUST 16 5:16 PM

A country as far from us as the entwining bands of space and time,
yet as near as the very atoms shaping our heartstrings, runs beside
this world like a clear, crystal-blue stream.
But here we skirt the underside of glory in lifelong
exile, longing, even if we are unaware of this pang, to
cross back in and roam that parallel country once again. . .

AUGUST 17 5:20 PM CONT. FROM ABOVE

. . .but we cannot get in. We beat our fists against the door of glory
but it will not budge—not yet. So we must content ourselves to
imagine—to perceive through the veil and siphon out the beauty of that
other country in art and word and song. We mold shadowy copies that soon
crumble into disrepair, yet still we cannot appease the ache. Yet we keep on
knocking for one day that veil shall be shorn back and the door will open at last
and we will enter in, becoming one with the beauty that so long
haunted our imaginations. Further up and further in will
be the chorus until we reach the world within the world
where beauty himself reigns o'er his garden Kingdom. And all
our creations will grow as spurs off the worlds when all is made new.

AUGUST 18 8:43 AM

The paths you've laid for me, Lord, have wound like streams
running to the sea from the doorframes of more homes and cities than I
care to count. And now, somehow those very paths have led me here, here
where tomorrow I must pack up my life and move once again. Just this time
onto a campus. I fear what lies ahead because the path twists out
of my sight. Yet I pray, oh Pathlayer, that you would grant me the
grace to follow regardless of where it might lead.

AUGUST 19 8:16 PM

A steeple rises against the dusk: white planking, gray frames,
green domes, slowly paled to rose-gold by the blazing saffron
behind. Like an Ebenezer raised to call the corners of creation
to worship the painter of every setting and every rise
and to welcome incarnate Mystery into its pillared sanctuary, it invites the dusk and its Maker to soak into the floorboards and hail the day of His return.

AUGUST 20 3:35 PM

I stand at a crossroads, in a place of in-between-ness.
It is not an evil country, scarred by tyrants or veins of bloody fire. Nor
is it a fair land, threaded by blue-quilt streams and forested by alpine
green. It is gray, desolate, barren, but for the languid wind. It is a place in which

many have found themselves. A place with no signpost but that which points to Home.

AUGUST 21 1:33 PM

Light from the open windows and a glow from the lamp
rise glad and golden to adorn the covers of all these books with
royal beams. They themselves are individual motes of light
refracted
and falling from the mind of the Author King, burrowing down
and condensing yet again into this tale resting on my desk.

AUGUST 22 6:10 PM

We summon and sail upon the tide of story as sub-creators of our
Maker's throne. Each of our little creations swirl madly around His
feet like flecks of golden grain kicked up as dust in the
stride of the King. Those blessed feet that bled and bleed into
our art, cleansing us in death that the tales we tell might live by His
breath.

AUGUST 23 11:05 AM

Give me strength, my God, that I may endure.
For my shoulders are weary, I am sore at soul, my eyes droop
with hours of unshed sleep, time and tide have come against me.
But you, oh Lord of my fathers, are a bulwark and a rock to
which I run, a bastion that will ne'er cave to frost nor fire.
And within the folds of your hovering wings, I might find the rest I
long for.

AUGUST 24 12:25 PM

I went to my college's dining hall today dressed as a praying mantis (no, this is not a joke). I didn't pull the lime-green costume from my closet, of course, thinking, "well, today seems like a mantis sort of day." It was given me as penance for a vile and dastardly crime and I wore it with as much solemnity as I could muster for the most holy of all insects. I don't even have a deep reflection tied to this story; just thought I might as well preserve the memory.

AUGUST 25 5:18 PM

Oh Lord, how often and how fervently have I beseeched your mercy to grace this sin-sick soul, yet now I seek your forbearance for offenses I have never considered, and I lay upon the altar every wrong I pretend I don't commit: for the coolness of my love and the slackness of my compassion, forgive this treacherous soul. For turning a blind eye to my suffering brother, for enacting injustice by refusing to act for the cause of justice, forgive this treacherous soul. For these and countless others that stand arrayed in a condemning host, forgive, oh God, this treacherous soul.

AUGUST 26 5:44 PM

Silence has gathered beneath the ancient stones of Graves Hall. The shadows of golden, windswept leaves waver against the forest green carpet pooling on the floor. I myself sit in a chair saturated by an upwelling

of light tinged orange by the stained glass window grinning a half dome
and dressed with gleaming petals. Through the arching windows overhead,
I can see the turrets of Dimnent soar to touch a summer-blue sky.
Peace is here in the throes of silence; the Spirit is here in his hushing breath.

AUGUST 27 6:47 PM

Even when I'm worn weary with engagements and
gatherings and cares, may you still grant me unmerited grace
to love well those who cross my path, to engage with their humanity,
to gather their stories into my own, to care truly and deeply for the divine
narrative that ordained the overlapping of our lives this very moment, this very place.

AUGUST 28 9:05 AM

If I close my eyes in the cool summer's breeze that billows
about me, I find there a symphony of aromas: the smell
of grass, of growing things, of night draining into the bowl of dawn.
I breathe the slow exhalation of trees; I breathe the air fringed with
lime and over and above it all like a prophecy of
coming kingdoms is the sweet, woody scent of autumn.

AUGUST 29 8:26 AM

I come again into the peace of stillness, into that language which trees and moors know so well, into that wild tongue that man has long misplaced and forgotten how to speak. This arboreal witness outside my window rebukes my momentary troubles with each
branching leaf. She deals, after all, in the economy of centuries, yet has learned to maintain this peace of stillness,
This stillness of rest, this rest of love.

AUGUST 30 12:45 PM

Softly and tenderly, Jesus is calling, calling me to cradle with care every heart that crosses my path. Like the heart of that person sitting beside me in my literature class who seemed so open to the mystery of faith but still carries questions and hurts that I could not touch. Help me, oh Christ, to be as an emissary unto these—these broken seekers, these ragged exiles searching for a land.

AUGUST 31 2:14 PM

This ancient tree with hair of thin, green leaves and the shadows she dapples on the golden grass, she is beloved in your court. The flower beds and birdsong around this laughing fountain are like choirs and carpets in this cathedral of creation. And help me to remember that even the man standing shirtless and vacant-eyed a distance away as he mutters to an audience only he can see is also an exile of Eden and a beloved courtier of the King of Kings.

IX

September

SEPTEMBER 1 1:43 PM

My life right now is uncertain, leaving a world behind.
These tears well from deep in my heart, this song will never die.
I don't know what I will gain, but all I know is you are there,
I'm looking to your heart right now to lead me on and show me the way.
I don't know what I will lose but without a doubt I'll see you move,
still my heart aches with all the doubt, I'm looking to you right now.

SEPTEMBER 2 9:06 AM

Oh would that all mankind in their bustling, clamoring, nose to the grindstone way, might learn to partake, if but for a moment, in the Shepherd's good rest. Of the lush meadows smelling sweetly of sun and dew, of the cool waters drenching parched throats with grace. May we all learn to walk in the wake of our Shepherd because any path beside this rambles trench-side to the abode of wolves.

SEPTEMBER 3 3:50 PM

Shadows on the floor cast by light produced by a distant star,
sent spiraling down into the pillars of space, away through
our atmosphere, before then falling golden upon wind-blown
leaves, then between the particles of a windowpane, at last
to rest like a gilded whisper upon a green carpet.

SEPTEMBER 4 9:09 AM

If your love, oh Christ, is truly a wellspring and my heart a waiting
vessel, then flow into me. May I run over this day with such an
outrageous joy, with such an implausible kindness, with such a
scandalous disregard for what others may think to themselves about me,
that all with whom my path crosses might see and know that you are God.

SEPTEMBER 5 12:36 PM

Come behold the wondrous mystery: Maker incarnate, God in flesh
among us and with us, Immanuel, Messiah, there in the beginning,
Word in the wilderness come to die, turning death backward
and inside out, shattering stone tables, bringing heaven to the brink of earth,
dying that death might die, and living that life might invade.

SEPTEMBER 6 12:45 PM

Shockwaves. They pulse through creation, radiating like bands
of song from Skull Hill where heaven and earth, so long rent,
met and fused in mythic flesh those two thousand years ago.
Shockwaves. They rumble still, like rings rippling out from the place
where a stone skimmed water; for now, we live in the chaos of the splash,
but soon we will fold into the ripples themselves and then go further beyond.

SEPTEMBER 7 6:18 PM

On the one side: a gracious saint, lips dripping with praise,
eyes golden with trust in his Maker's goodness. On the other:
a raging child rampaging madly when he doesn't get his way;
foul, hot-headed, demanding, and utterly, utterly selfish.
Who will unite these two hemispheres within me?
Who can bridge this divide and make me at last one man?

SEPTEMBER 8 9:14 AM

What is it about speeding down the open road that so enthralls
me with the world? Is there a wanderlust seeded like maple somewhere
I have forgotten to look, a yearning to roam those eternal foothills
that wakes when I watch groves of sun-soaked trees and
speckled roads and misty pastures blur by the window?

SEPTEMBER 9 4:50 PM

Sometimes, ever so rarely, my mind is allowed to soar beyond
the wavering borders of time and take root amid the starry steeps.
I am seized, for the grain of a moment within a larger moment, by the
sheer wonder that I stand on a rock hurtling around a
burning sun—myself only a small pinprick of life in a
never-ending whorl of galaxies. I tremble then my mind returns.

SEPTEMBER 10 9:38 AM

Birdsong heralds the crowning of this golden dawn.
A gilded pearl pushes up from the eastern sea to imbue
a flaxen hue to the tree's dewy hair and the sloping, squirrel-haven
lawn. Creation flames and flickers, soars and sings,
lifts leafy hands to praise the Son rising with the dawn.

SEPTEMBER 11 9:45 AM

Where do the seconds go once they have funneled down into
momentary consciousness, then vanished again as if they had never
been?
An hourglass of time, perhaps, an antechamber of sand
secreted unseen below this thin passage upon which man is ever
perched.
It seems, then, that imagination is perception, that life is memory.

SEPTEMBER 12 1:45 PM

Torrents of rain are bred in the heights and they pour down
like a brood of blunted needles, like a horde of dull-blade ice,

tossing the trees into a fright of green, lashing the windows
as with glassy glaze, whipping the water into a frenzy of
waves. And still the clouds open to bid autumn in.

SEPTEMBER 13 4:45 PM

Gazing up, up into the reaches of this tree: layers of thin rafter wood
raising rustling praise to the sapphire-bright heavens.
Sunlight filters down between each supple leaf and they blush, tinged
golden as if beneath the gilded thumb of Midas, ruffling like the pages
of a book, bearing arboreal stories in their glowing veins.

SEPTEMBER 14 8:06 PM

On a walk alone in Centennial Park, I stumble across
a tree, an ancient Ent who stands proudly beside the fountain.
This, perhaps, is the grandfather of the green. His noble trunk,
the color of pencil shavings, stands like a pillar wound of wooden sinews,
his hoary head drooping to listen to the laughter of water.

SEPTEMBER 15 2:02 PM

Where are the singing elves of Rivendell? I wonder as I stand here.
Where is the sound of harps strummed by fingers lithe and limber, their
toes in blue water, their hair in the river dew? I wish that I could leap
headlong into the river and suck fire-frost water into my lungs

and find that I float like an acorn husk upon streams that flow out of ticking
clocks and into another forest where pines tower like steeples
and lullaby mist crackles in our throats.

SEPTEMBER 16 9:29 AM

I have found a sort of indoor arbor, with domed roof like the sky,
straining for a pinnacle illumined by a sphere of gold
that beams gladly upon the wooden paneling and wide windows
and restful trees. Like the spokes of a wagon wheel, like the face of a
grandfather clock, I feel as if I could turn back time in this place.

SEPTEMBER 17 11:55 AM

Teach my soul where and how I might seek you.
Truly, oh Lord, you dwell in unapproachable light, a light
that heals and makes new, yet also strips sinew from bone and
delves painfully into dark caverns I wish not to roam.
Yet I long for you, I yearn to look full in your face. Who will lead
me into this light that I might at once be blinded yet also come to see?

SEPTEMBER 18 1:34 PM

Charlatans and scoundrels arrayed in rows of shattered saints,
sacredness in slobber, holiness in hovels, peace in profane,
first last, last first, children emperors, monarchs as fools,
God become flesh, not to rule, but to die; villains repented, rogues redeemed:
that is what the Kingdom of heaven will be.

SEPTEMBER 19 8:38 PM

Oh that I might live each day, each moment, each micro-minute
between moments, as if the world were truly saturated with magic,
as if the high poetry that ushered creation from the womb of deep space still
rumbles through the earth, as if I am forgiven, as if I am beloved,
as if I and all things will one day be redeemed.

SEPTEMBER 20 9:21 AM

Small town America spans before me—miles of rusty grain rushing out from
this narrow thread of road like the undulating sprawl of
a sunset-blushing sea. Patches of scraggly trees—worn out,
faded barns, fenced in plots where horses graze, sun blazing
down, ranch-style homes, tractors rumbling out into distant fields.

SEPTEMBER 21 6:12 PM

The water wells are deep here. This is the wood between the worlds
in which leaping, swan-like, into the drenching ice might carry me as a
tufted dandelion seed to worlds beyond number. Two marble-blue eyes rove
the windswept mountains, and children cast stones into the rippling mirror
like coins cast, wishing, into a well. The banks are quiet and green as clover.
I cast a coin and wish—four leaves lucky—for the mountains to break into

laughter, for the stories to one day come true, for the
pine trees to tremble with song, for all things at last to be new.

SEPTEMBER 22 1:13 PM

The colors have begun to change. Each wondrous leaf is woven
with symphonies of light and chlorophyll as they shed their
priestly vestments of royal green to bear instead autumnal
garments.
Garments that whisper of beauty before death, yet
proclaim the eventual reversal of death back into beauty.

SEPTEMBER 23 1:22 PM

The veil feels thin here, as if I could reach through and feel
my hands bathed in a flow of rushing glory, as if I could listen with
weeping
ears and humming eyes to a lost melody I have long yearned to join.
The veil feels thin here as if I could at last break through and
dance upon the dewy hills soaring upward into Aslan's Country.

SEPTEMBER 24 12:47 PM

Forgive me, Father, for I have sinned against you in thought, word,
and deed,
again by what I have done, and again by what I have left undone.
With each act of treason I enact against your Throne,
I feel as if I am twisting myself methodically into a warped shadow
of your design.
Are these not the gnarled crown of thorns drawing chaplets of
blood from your brow?

SEPTEMBER 25 4:56 PM

A high, keening rise of notes, tremulous like the gasps of a weeping lover, bending as teardrops around my listening ears as it goes. . . then it recedes down the scale, golden-brown like honey flowing from a riven comb. Crestfallen, a bereaved heart, a sighing princess, now away suddenly, following swiftly the arc of all history into hope.

SEPTEMBER 26 4:47 PM

Each person I pass are radiant princes, or star-bright princesses—immortal
creatures majestic and beloved, an assembly of priests with the flowers
of song tied around their girdles, and the branches of story adorning
their brows. They are shimmering words falling from the lips of the Word in the beginning.
Baptize my vision, therefore, that I might see this every day as true.

SEPTEMBER 27 4:53 PM

Stories in starlight, dreams in dewdrops, magic in mountains, histories in hedgerows, wonder in waterfalls, mystery in maelstroms, songs in seas, poems in peonies, secrets
in snowfall, prayers in ponds, rhymes in rivers, and good in everything.

SEPTEMBER 28 11:51 AM

Creations groans. I can feel the pang of all that is lost racing beneath
my feet from tree root to stalk of grass to branch to breeze then into
the sky: a weeping blue. This is our temple, whose ground we have raped.
This is our claim, whose waters we've fouled with engines of progress,
regress, rather, from beauty to broken, from peace to pain. This is our shoddy,
puppet kingdom teetering madly on the precipice of the pillage
and purge of all we have inflicted upon this, our slobbered-on chapel.

SEPTEMBER 29 11:57 AM

The world clamors, "extremes! Extremely extreme! Extreme culture,
extreme politics, extreme division," on and on it rages, sour and embattled,
fracturing a human race in factions of plastered promises and oily sneers.
But the silence, that ever-present, drowned out stillness, yet whispers o'er her
abode: "peace! Peaceful peace! Peace like a river. Peace after the storm. Peace
undergirding this pain until pain is pierced by peace and peace adorns
the tender brow of the Prince of all Peace."

SEPTEMBER 30 11:49 AM

They say the Kingdom is on the move and that it lingers in the places which bear its Maker's mark. But why, oh Lord, is it so hard to see? Why does the Holy Ghost seem to flit away out of view whenever I turn my head to look? Why are the things of heaven seen best from out the corner of my eye?

X

October

OCTOBER 1 12:13 PM HICKORY IN AUTUMN I

All is silent as a snow-swept rise, the skies wander from
eddying white to lights of blue and simmering gold,
as cold as a breathless curtain of stars. It's here, as the magic
hour slowly fades and braids soft blushes through the rustling leaves, that
wreathes of rollicking laughter seem to stream from the throat of an autumnal King.

OCTOBER 2 12:14 PM HICKORY IN AUTUMN II

For the gentle hill is the swell of His brow, like a crown arrayed
there, a chaplet of rose. In throes of pale fire, his breath like
the breeze, the trees are his staff, the meadows his cloak.
The world is sleeping and the leaves must fall, the scrawl of death's touch stains
all of creation; yet he hastens, this gladsome, laughing King,
for springtime to flower and newness to waken.

OCTOBER 3 1:46 PM

Autumn is pluming up against the world like breakers on a shallow reef. Currents move coolly across my skin like the touch of gentle water. Rustling trees drop brands of pale fire into the heart of the sky and there they billow endlessly like sparks shaken from the afternoon sun until all creation seems to laugh aloud with the promise of fall.

OCTOBER 4 3:47 PM

An autumnal fire-spirit winks from a dappling of sighing leaves. Her hair glows like the liquid core of an orange coal and it flows down her gentle shoulders in a veil of wandering sparks. A gossamer gown of swirling gold billows sweetly around her bare ankles and when the breeze wends its bright course to murmur in her elfin ears, she lifts the winds as a silken brush and weaves blushes into the trees.

OCTOBER 5 8:12 AM

Apple picking. Rows of bell-shaped trees overlook a terrace
of grape vines. Green orbs, rosy lips, hiding beneath dewy leaves.
The smell of autumn air, the feel of numb fingers, the sunlight
filtering down around us soft and pale, like a whisper.
Beloved family. Falling leaves. Crisp breeze. Warm memories.
Apple picking.

OCTOBER 6 3:52 PM

Come to the country where clouds are like ships sailing starboard
and starbound before a full-masted wind
like sprigs of cotton, like shorn wool pure and nebulous, rising
ever upward and onward, soaring beyond the walls of time,
deep into the wells of space, then out and down again like a rocket.

OCTOBER 7 6:26 PM

The first shy colors of the year lie crimson upon every branch.
Wind and day's end rake together the treetops, feeding the
dewy earth with fallen embers. A wind of autumn flakes billows
like sawdust before the feet of the coming night. Beyond this gray mantle,
the great Tide-bringer wakes and the wind-blown stars flare once more to sing.

OCTOBER 8 5:02 PM

Please let me make something beautiful, something that whispers that
poets are ever underfoot, that death is an unnatural perversion,
that the darkness will one day pass, that the stories are true, that fairy
land is nearer than we ever hoped to dream, that the dawn is speeding swiftly
on the heels of night. Infuse my creation with a snarl of tangled sunrays.

OCTOBER 9 11:13 PM

Soul-sick and weary, I travel this road rent ragged by the feet of many wayward
Apostles. This is the road to Nineveh, to Damascus, to Jerusalem, riding
Under a blood moon. This is the haunt of sinners and saints, all loved and
Lost, forgiven and forsaken, saved and shamed, broken yet beloved.

OCTOBER 10 6:23 PM

There is a place I have longed for many tear-stricken nights,
yet it is not the place where I stand—this little castle overlooking
a tiny green sea that froths sharply in plumes of shredded foam
at a threading dike of asphalt. This is a mirror-realm, refracting from behind
glory the promise of an at-last place, where the castles
span flowery meadows and the waters are ever sweet.

OCTOBER 11 5:01 PM

Restless, ever restless, she flows into the borders of time,
eyes bright with liquid glass, blustery leaves embedded in her
footfalls, hair white as frost and wreathed as with ice.
She rustles her silvern body through the rust-laden leaves,
weary of pummeling yet restless still for the day in which rest will flow
into her flowing, give feathers to her steel, and weave her back to breeze.

OCTOBER 12 1:45 PM

Poetry limned like liquid silver flowing in dewy tides
from the inkwell of the Lord Poet. Thin downstrokes:
the faint rain of golden leaves. Thick upstrokes:
sun-speckled trees drinking deeply of pooling light.
The poem of creation playing itself out like a rumor of lost Eden.

OCTOBER 13 1:49 PM

Red barns keep watch o'er stubbled fields of pale green
beneath a sky wheeling with an oblivion of clouds.
Pastures roll with the furor of wind-tossed seas, their
emerald borders subsumed with trees touched by gold.
Beneath each slumbering colossus, a ring of muted yellow.

OCTOBER 14 10:43 AM

I imagine a trove of white stones piled in a heavenly courtyard
reaching higher than mountains, humming with
luminosity as if swollen with stars, glowing with melody like music
boxes dripping birdsong. On each stone is carved a name; a name that far
outstrips our old souls even as Everest soars beyond a crumbling molehill.

OCTOBER 15 2:35 PM

I bow my head in sorrow as experts report embers of deep pain.
There, the very ground our Lord once tread, is now riddled with exploding shells.

Both sides wrong, the holy land rendered unholy: raped women, beheaded babies,
mutilated men on hills where miracles were once enacted. I voice my grieving
vespers through this autumn air: oh Christ who suffers with us, hold us close,
while we wait and weep for Jerusalem and watch for it at last to descend.

OCTOBER 16 12:03 PM

Oh Christ, who knows what it is to grieve, walk with me here
amid this sad exile. My lips are smudged with darkness, my eyes
brim over with tears, my head is bowed and bloodied. How I yearn
for you, my King! It is for your country that I earnestly seek, yet I wander still
through shadow, veiled from glory, scraping my knees as I stumble and roam.

OCTOBER 17 7:55 PM

The world rolls back into black seas like the eye of a dreaming lover,
or a droplet of dew falling into shadow from a rain-dappled leaf.
The sun, like a ripening capsule, bursts apart into a scattering
of seeds, of sand tumbling across Abraham's beaches, of fireflies caught
and blown away upward by a high wind into the wildness of firmamental breakers.

OCTOBER 18 1:04 PM

A season of mist and rusty gold, when the fields are crimson
and the breezes are cold, rustling through hedgerows and willowing
boughs, nudging autumn leaves to open old wings, then settle to sleep
on sloping thatch-eaves. The bend in the road is a yellow-leafed veil,
and by cottage trees goes the golden-green trail.

OCTOBER 19 2:46 PM

From behind my opened window, I can see a palate of still
colors: the blushing pink of crabapples, the black of darting squirrels,
a mane of forest green, lightening to lime at the Ent's shaggy pinnacle.
Beyond: a swath of brooding crimson, accented by sunset's
pumpkin orange, followed at last by a dome of rustling gold.

OCTOBER 20 9:36 PM

I feel a bit like a dried-up well, a quill pen that has run out of
ink. I cannot think of anything to write; there is nothing clever or
witty or especially spiritual about any thought that passes through my pen.
They seem to drift languidly along from one thing to the next—tired, aimless, unfocused.
Anchor them instead to yourself, Father, lest they stray ever away.

OCTOBER 21 10:03 AM

In bough and bole a prayer is shaped like falling light through stirring
leaves. A wild supplication, solemn and ragged, rustles as wind
in high branches. The woodland mourns its ancient loves, now gone away
or locked in rings. In every loss, in every spring, a low, lamenting song
seems to bleed from autumn leaves, a song that bids us enter returning time,
that calls as a lonesome bride to an ancestor never fully known,
that rehearses this earth through centuries long to pray again that far-off song.

OCTOBER 22 2:29 PM

I venture into the wildness beyond maps, armed with naught but
my fallow pen and a poem that murmurs like a blackbird in the crook of
my soul. With grist for the mill, and pearls 'mid the grit,
I embark into land foreign and fey to quietly stalk the silvery vapor of
epiphany, to ready a landing strip for the descending Muse,
to reach bare-handed into the blood and gasping of labor
and midwife a shape, a language, a poem into the world.

OCTOBER 23 1:35 PM

The sky's vast palm overflowed this afternoon with a faint marbling
of flurries. They roamed down and out of the high country like gentle
fireflies wandering lost from mountain pastures. The first glimpse

of winter's steady approach, a momentary aligning of the hem of her snow-satin garment with the sleeping lips of husband earth.

OCTOBER 24 12:37 PM

Stories are not only contained in books, or recorded in flowing script;
stories are there in the ribs of each leaf, running like music
melted and molten from stem to branch to crystalline air.
For creation whispers "green and gold," that ancient, holy tale,
that ragged, winsome poetry that lifts us up and through the veil.

OCTOBER 25 2:33 PM

I sit by the window, my elbows on the wooden sill,
and watch the first snow churn madly in the shrouded heights.
It rages, yet utterly silent; it burns, yet is not warm; it billows like sawdust,
yet has no wings; it piles along the streets and frosts each little
leaf; it nips at my nose, this wild, raw cold, yet as it falls
serenely as whispers, I sense something deeper and here voice my vespers.

OCTOBER 26 5:12 PM

Rolled in autumn vestments, this lost Ent-wife stands, her leaves
golden as apples, orange as pumpkins, green as the core of
a candle's flame, doused in drifting beads of snowfall, her branches
lined with ice. She wavers steadily as the frozen breeze braids through
her hair, freeing a sudden rush and rain of snow and falling leaves.

OCTOBER 27 3:03 PM

I am weary in this afternoon hour, weary of I know not what.
For the sun is glimmering in fields of blue, the high leaves
are stirred by ancient wind, the ground is arrayed with embers
of falling red; of what have I to be weary? Will you, my King,
grant me your peace until when at last this weariness will cease?

OCTOBER 28 4:43 PM

A solitary thrush perched in yonder tanglewood of boughs
surveys a world shaped by wind. Her downy breast is pale rose,
as if her feathers altered hue at the eating of crabapples, as if perhaps
she spilled upon her frock blushed wine at a sparrow's wedding banquet.
Then, she lifts wing and soars into the undulating blue, her
breast as bright as a berry tucked between sprigs of holly.

OCTOBER 29 1:38 PM

Leaves, shadowed, drifting down, down, nudged by breeze,
caught by currents, enveloped by gravity, spiraling groundward
like bloodstained sparks coughed up by a fire, only to trail
brokenly down again as worn-out ashes, faded in death. Leaves, lightened,
falling finally into brown, till spring doth return in golden and green.

OCTOBER 30 4:32 PM

And yet, yet these fallen leaves, golden slowly browned, these
harbingers of death, skeletal branches rattling like bones,
ever proclaim through crackling lips a keening hymn, as mournful
as a tomb riven with ivy and age, as hopeful as a flicker in a young
mother's eyes, for new light yet drips on these aged leaves.

OCTOBER 31 5:36 PM

Here on this last night of October, I reflect on two things: your goodness and
my brokenness. Over and over again, Lord, I have gone blatantly against your Word
and will, and I now ask forgiveness for all the evil I have done, and equally for all
the goods I might have done, yet failed to do. In the nearing winter, God and King, may you, by
your ever-abiding mercies, heal what has been broken and restore what has been lost.

XI

November

NOVEMBER 1 10:27 AM

This morning, when I rose from my bed and went to the window,
I saw the dark tree line draped with wreaths of billowing mist
that moved and rippled like branches stirred by the white lady
winter.
And while I watch the fog swell fluidly about oaken knees,
I feel that the world roars of mystery this day. Then the morning
turns and the mist fades.

NOVEMBER 2 10:50 AM

A thousand leaves have fallen and they float across
the lawn like burning embers of snow. And I also
am like a shaking leaf clinging to a withering branch of life
from which I must one day fall. Yet Lord, let me be like
an evergreen that even in death I will yet point ever heavenward
and hopeward.

NOVEMBER 3 6:38 PM

This song rises to me out of the settling dusk like
a stream of pale water rustling through autumn leaves.
The trees stand solemn in these brisk November days and
they seem to breathe ever deeply, perhaps remembering
a time before the buzz of the highway drowned out the evening.

NOVEMBER 4 8:56 PM

The gray mantle of clouds above me parted only for a moment,
but in that breath's span, I could see a faint glimmer,
or better yet, a steady sigh of light as though a luminous sphere
of ice had wandered through space and decided by some eternal wisdom to
remind me once more that beauty spans forever beyond the darkness.

NOVEMBER 5 9:40 AM

A soft suggestion of breeze whispers through the treetops
and shakes loose the last remaining leaves.
It nips at my fingers and pulls on my hair, but when I
breathe it in, something about its autumnal sweetness
resurrects the golden memory of a day in my childhood.

NOVEMBER 6 4:55 PM

I see the King's goodness in this hallowed court of witnesses.
It's as if all creation is a jewel and each shining facet
refracts the good pleasure of its Maker into the sanctuary of the eye.

There is peace here in this wild mystery. Is it
in the birds soaring across the dome of sky or the
spattering of golden light upon this restful tree?

NOVEMBER 7 4:41 PM

This world is swollen with splendor and pregnant with
traces of slumbering magic. I see it in the ice-bearded blue
of the cathedral bounds of sky above me; there are shapes
in the heights and pluming footfalls of color and just for a moment,
I wonder if I have seen in the cloudy steeps the passing form of the one who made it all.

NOVEMBER 8 9:24 PM

"Why are the things of heaven seen best from out the corner of my eye?"
This I wrote in September—the honest cry of a young man
searching sincerely for rumors of the King, yet in the months since, I have come
to learn that the peripheral is central, the central peripheral,
and by stillness, all on the edges can be teased out, or wooed
into the foreground until our vision itself is drenched by holiness.

NOVEMBER 9 9:19 PM

Last night, I sat before a blazing fire as snow battered the window panes.
Tonight, I wandered through a darkling woodland
wreathed by bands of white and gold. I know not yet where

next eventide might sweep these weary feet, but this story in my hands
is like a bridge between worlds and might whisk me anywhere.

NOVEMBER 10 11:28 AM

I call myself a writer, and yet every word I scratch down is a battle
waged between my frail human will and a dark, unholy resistance that
seeks to rend apart all that tastes of glory. I call myself a writer, and yet
I am struck, as I look upward at the breathless bounds of sky, with the
tearful, joyous realization that I could never dream of describing that.

NOVEMBER 11 8:34 PM

The Lady of the North breathed today; as tendrils of creeping cold
ducked sheepishly in and out of the trees, I looked up
and saw in the skies, as though in a wide, pale pane of water,
the icy, gray coldness of each frosty blade of grass
reflected there in the swirling, subtle silver of the autumn-swollen clouds.

NOVEMBER 12 8:05 PM

I woke up this morning and scrambled to the window.
My breaths formed banks of fog on the glass, and I saw,
almost luminous against the dark, brooding sky, a sudden
Thrill of peaceful white flurries. My heart swelled with
longing as though I were a little boy watching the first snow of the year.

NOVEMBER 13 9:45 AM

It began in the dawn-streaked sky: flake upon flake of silent,
wind-blown snow falling from high storehouses and drifting
gently upon our field-fringed home. They fluttered like
soft white birds with sprigs of holly clutched in their beaks—
rumors of Christmas, signposts pointed toward the Kingdom.

NOVEMBER 14 5:06 PM

The warmth of this house as the weather turns cold,
the old, woody scent that rises from this page,
the sudden swell of music as supper cooks upstairs,
the verse soaring from Scripture like a candle in a cave:
these all, and still more, are dear treasures of the King.

NOVEMBER 15 5:00 PM

Are there little stories engraved within each snowflake?
Are there tiny tales in the veins of every leaf?
For when that delicious, crisp air begins to stir through the forest, it's as if a window is opened to a wooded vale of worlds in my mind
whose histories I may record and whose chronicles I might one day weave.

NOVEMBER 16 2:52 PM

He is a God of love and thunder, of fire and water, not safe,
not tame, but inconceivably Good. His love is like

the snowfall: reckless and raging as it swirls madly from the gray-blue
heights above, yet hushed as a whisper, white as pure linen,
a refractor of light into the dark tanglewoods of soul and nature.

NOVEMBER 17 10:20 PM

Who can say that I'm an author, that I write of things living
only in the hallowed halls of imagination, when I feel like a
passenger in this story I claim to tell? I am nothing but a voyager on this
ship. I am not the captain—for the wheel is now in the hands of a character
I thought I made up, but I see now is more real than many others around me.

NOVEMBER 18 4:05 PM

You've orchestrated our world like a heart-wrenching song
and the keys to unlocking its countless cupboards of mystery
may sometimes be found only in music. For when notes
bend the air and melodies soar homesick through my chest, I
realize with a laugh of wonder that music is truly more potent than
anything that keeps me awake.

NOVEMBER 19 5:11 PM

Help me, oh Lord, to listen to my life. To experience every
sense, every fleeting flame of moment, for the wide,
fathomless mystery it is. For there at the heart
of every passing second, is a hidden and holy sanctuary in which

only the Maker may dwell. Help me, oh Lord, to bend my ear to
that secret space.

NOVEMBER 20 9:24 PM

To all the poets who built a boat and sailed into the great unknown,
who told the darkness of endless hope and marched to face their foes alone.
To all the poets who raised a sword, girded in the armor of song and rhyme,
who befriended notes and strummed their chords, who danced upon the threads of time.
To all the poets who saw beyond and kindled verse onto blank pages,
who wielded words like wizard's wands, who wept with love of their creations.
To all the poets I've never met who saw the truth within each moment,
who carved words down with tears and sweat, you've made me too into a poet.

NOVEMBER 21 8:21 AM

How easy it is, oh Lord, in the roiling currents of each day,
to see myself as an all-important entity, a little god who must
grasp and strain and extend to feed my own ravenous belly. Rarely do I
name myself rather a frail member of the bride's body; rarely do I see
those around me as fellow pilgrims on this road toward glory.

NOVEMBER 22 1:56 PM

Sometimes I wish I noticed more; I wish I saw the world
as it truly is: a vast book scribed through with wonder and adventure,
a book in which I am a character. I wish I noticed
the intensity of the grass's green or the vibrant blue
of the wide, deep sky, or the patchwork of browns in the stand of trees.

NOVEMBER 23 5:18 PM

The distant horizon is set ablaze by eddies of orange and currents
of burning red; the wispy smoke-breaths of cloud above
are plum-purple and fringed by shades of blushing rose.
Then higher still: light yellows and faded golds all below an expanse of blue.
It's as if the sky is a canvas and God stoops to sketch the sunset.

NOVEMBER 24 7:32 PM

I give you thanks for my family and friends, for the laughter
shared around the dinner table, for the scent of good
things baking in the oven, for the Christmas lights upon our
snowy gables. I praise you, Lord, for these and still more.
They say the prayers of the saints rise about your throne as incense.
I wonder today if they smell a bit like pumpkin pie.

NOVEMBER 25 2:06 PM

The late autumn sky is pale as a pearl hidden and held
fast by the hands of a cloudy miser. It swirls

like a cosmos alive in shy shades—powder blue
and breathy pink and tender yellow—a pastel of
high beauty seen only when I look upward from the sallow earths around me.

NOVEMBER 26 3:17 PM

From India to South Bend to Springfield to Holland,
I'd never be fooled into thinking I belong to this place.
I am rather a sojourner, a pilgrim of a country I
can scarcely even remember, and yet I strive on for
that far haven. Wandering, yet found.

NOVEMBER 27 3:38 PM

Her voice has been ravaged by years of illness,
but they tell me she once used to sing like an angel.
And as she pressed "play" on the battered tape recorder,
a voice high and beautiful rang out from the speakers,
and I realized that for the first time I had truly heard my grandmother sing.

NOVEMBER 28 4:14 PM

If the trees before me now could tell all the stories
their fattening rings have locked away, surely I'd hear tales of
pain and sorrow and betrayal and loss and death, for these indeed
are the realities of this floundering world. But set next to life, all this grieving
would scarcely fill a thimble. So the trees also preach joy and wonder and peace.

NOVEMBER 29 5:29 PM

Lord, as we adorn the tree and unbox our Christmas decorations,
we affirm that something unimaginable has happened in time and space:
God himself entered the frail frame of man to dwell
among us and to open up for us the path to his eternal Kingdom.
Fill this home, Lord, for there is room here as we rehearse that coming, sounding joy.

NOVEMBER 30 4:03 PM

The restless wind howls around me, clutching me in
arms of frost. A great limb from the sinewy trees lining
our yard has fallen like a broken warrior on the field of battle,
and I realize, as the trees groan menacingly in the gale, how utterly
weak am I and how violent, yet wonderful, God's world can be.

XII

December

DECEMBER 1 6:20 PM

As the sun sank below the waters of the horizon like a
storm-ravaged ship, it seemed
for a moment, for a tentative breath, that a pillar of red
light stood tall above the skyline like a spire of color
before the encroaching dusk swallowed it back like it had never
been at all.

DECEMBER 2 1:47 PM

Today, I heard him sing about Hosea and Gomer: the prophet and
the prostitute.
Their unlikely union a sign to Israel of their unfaithfulness
to God. And as I thought about that backward story,
I realized how freely how I give my attentions to oher clamoring
hosts.
I am Gomer, the prostitute bride of Christ. Forgive me, dear Lord!

DECEMBER 3 4:58 PM

To all the dreamers who cleared the trails, and put signposts within the ground,

who carried with them ancient tales to find things which had not been found.

To all the dreamers who spent their souls to see the ending of their fight,

who saw the end and reached their goal, who sprinkled the air around with light.

To all the dreamers who saw a need and strove to build a better place,

who saw ripe fields in a plain of weeds, who seasoned life with the salt of grace.

To all the dreamers I've never known, the lovers and the believers,

who saw new worlds in sheets of stone, you've made me too into a dreamer.

DECEMBER 4 5:31 PM

I don't know what's wrong with me. I'm tired of talking, tired of thinking,

tired of this broken mind. I feel so wretched—how could you ever love me?

My eyes are too dimmed to see your face, so I grope in the dark like a vile,

sightless beast in this rotting cave of a heart. Are you angry or merciful?

Gracious or ashamed? Help me to believe, oh God, lest I suffer alone.

DECEMBER 5 11:12 AM

The brown, wintry bracken that surrounded the footpath was all I saw
as my feet crunched in the gravel. Yet as I rounded a bend in the road, a
blue jay took flight before me in a sudden thrill of color, and it was as if the
Lord told me to consider the birds. And truly when I looked up and around, the steely
skies were in the throes of a high alchemy and praise God! for green was everywhere!

DECEMBER 6 4:39 PM

I have a confession to make. That last poem was a lie.
Yes, it really happened—the blue jay and high alchemy and
unexpected green—but did it happen yesterday? Short answer: no.
That happened today. I just failed to write yesterday, so I penned two today.
And I've done that for multiple poems throughout. My bad.

DECEMBER 7 2:38 PM

Everyone talks about the green of spring, the vivid emeralds
and flaming sages. But as I stand here on this porch—the wooden planks
beneath my feet not unlike the deck of some high-perched ship overlooking
a cold, green sea—I am struck with the feeling that perhaps winter greens

are the brightest of all when set beside the chilled background of gray and brown.

DECEMBER 8 5:20 PM

I give you, Lord, the chapter I wrote today. I am aware—all too aware—of
how fleeting and fallible my words truly are, but
fleeting and fallible is all I have to give. If it would please you, great Author of
life and Author of my life, hallow these hollow sentences, that they may shine with a beauty and a radiance that could never have come from me.

DECEMBER 9 12:08 PM

Teach me to number my days. For life can seem abiding if
I am not careful; in my veiled, disillusioned wisdom, I struggle to see each passing hour like a blade of grass: here today and tomorrow gone.
Therefore, my decisions must matter. Help me, Lord, to live this journey well,
that my daily choices might stretch like a newly paved road unto the courts of eternity.

DECEMBER 10 6:20 PM

Is it wrong to say that snow is silent? I suppose not, because
as it flutters from the clouds like icy tears flaking from star-ridden eyes,

it seems so soft and peaceful. And yet, I cannot help but remember the Psalms
and the countless times the poets imagine creation as a singing assembly. Could
it be that even snowfalls sing hallelujahs in silvern tongues beyond human ears?

DECEMBER 11 10:36 AM

May this calloused heart be replaced again with the heart of a child,
a heart that sees the world not for the shadow it is now,
but rather as the glory it will one day be. May I
see this world for what she truly is: a vast storybook opened
from horizon to horizon, in which turning day nears us still to the start of Chapter One.

DECEMBER 12 5:14 PM

I wonder how many people have taken the time to study a leaf.
I have. Call me strange if you wish, but they are truly remarkable.
The velvety softness between my fingers, the branching veins through which
light and life and water flow. It reminds me that I serve a God who allows something
as commonplace as a leaf to preach sermons to man of the power borne by simple beauty.

DECEMBER 13 5:37 PM

There's a wailing whisper building in the heavens, a flame is in the west.

For the bleeding clouds are like a sounding banner filled with murmuring breath.
For beyond them lies a country and above their burning ranks there rides a King.
And he comes to fill the nations, every corner of creation, to extend the invitation
to a Kingdom of salvation. It is rolling down the mountains, to the cold
and rolling fountains, from the trees and hills before us, to the high and hallowed
chorus that every tor and every forest echoes out like thunder for us
that lost melody our souls yet yearn to sing.

DECEMBER 14 5:06 PM

I praise you, my Maker, for the stillness that wells around me like
pools of rippling starlight, for the moments, however brief,
where I may hide myself within the cleft of mountains and simply be
as your quiet glory passes by. As these songs draw toward
a close, may I continue to seek stillness, for it is where your presence dwells.

DECEMBER 15 3:35 PM

A gray mantle of clouds cloaks the sky for the fourth day running.
That's what it's like here in Michigan during the winter. The lake to the west,
like a happy shearer and a rattling loom, churns out miles of thick fleece.
And people here complain about this grayness, but there's beauty there if only you'll
look: light, downy shades melting into swathes of frowning white.

For grays too are lovely, if only I see; reminds me somehow of
grace.

DECEMBER 16 11:09 AM

Lord, when I know not what else to write, let me simply
erupt in praise to you. I give thanks for this mid-December day, for
the domes of snow capping the bird feeder, for the ice-wands in the tree's
branching hair, for the woody scent of cedar and cinnamon swirling about
the glowing Christmas tree, for the glad tidings imbuing this most wonderful time of the year.

DECEMBER 17 1:31 PM

The Lord lifts the world by its corners and shakes it forward
and back, up and down, and the heavens respond with a laugh of praise.
The high storehouses where snows are gathered have burst like thunderheads over
this swath of earth and Lord smiles as he finishes his shaking.
The world is a snow globe in the palm of a ruddy-cheeked Craftsman.

DECEMBER 18 10:25 AM

This place is filled with laughter and love, tales told and carols sung,
with good smells and piles of gifts and hugs and every good
Christmas thing. These people around me are not just people,
we are a gladsome congregation, joyous migrants, light-hearted

pilgrims sharing these happy little moments on our journey to glory.

DECEMBER 19 10:31 AM

Away into the bushes garmented with white go the prints in the snow.
Little rabbit feet bounding carefree in the winter, soft exhalations
of warm breath spilling from twitching nostrils like the mists hovering
above a roasting turkey, then off again! running, leaping,
sitting once more all in this snowy playground of winter's good pleasure.

DECEMBER 20 9:41 AM

They say a blizzard is coming two nights from today,
just in time for a white Christmas. I'm an adult now, but
I'd be lying if I said I wasn't delighted. My little boy heart shivers
inside me at the promise of snow fluttering down on soft, tiny wings
as we feast and fellowship and carol our way through the storm.
All is as it should be.

DECEMBER 21 11:20 AM

The sun pushed through the slate-gray clouds for the
first time in weeks; it winks and beams against the snow:
atoms of light refracted from a million gleaming crystals.
And in each sudden flash of light, in each unexpected burst of gold,

I seem to hear the Father of Snows whisper, "My son, see how much I love you!"

DECEMBER 22 9:28 AM

The trees stand so still and silent against the pale sky.
The wisps of cloud are like flinders of stone glowing with a light contained
within themselves. Snow continues to blanket the earth,
sweeping through the forest, pushing under trees, and rolling over hills.
All is peace and praise here in this chapel of creation.

DECEMBER 23 10:51 AM PART ONE

Through this haze of years, I seem to see a dusty, fly-ridden
street clogged and stifled by many pressing bodies. There's a woman called Mary
somewhere in the center of this teeming mass of humanity; she sits
slumped over a donkey's bowed neck, gasping as labor pains
shear through her belly. Any minute, any minute the baby will come. She can feel
blood seeping into the rough, woolen garment that scratches relentlessly at her skin.
So hot! So dirty! So hard to breathe! The woman's betrothed, a man named Joseph,
lays a gentle hand on her knee, but she scarcely recognizes his touch. The pain grows.
The man bites his lip and looks desperately around. The inns are full
to bursting and they disgorge roiling guts of humankind into the streets.

"Damn this census," he growls. There seems to be only one place. The man guides his
skin-and-bones donkey down a narrow alley. He has heard that there are
stables in the stark cave country that runs the fringes of Bethlehem.
The woman groans. Any minute the baby will come. "Elohim, help us!" the man cries.

DECEMBER 24 12:46 PM PART TWO

The glaring sun has fallen behind the seething sky
giving way now to raw cold. Mary and Joseph
enter the drafty stable. The liquid eyes of a plodding cow turn to greet them, and
sheep push from their rickety pens likely in some misbegotten quest to
plead for scraps. The smell of animals fills the cold air; it
nips at the woman as she eases herself to the muddy floor with a whimper of
pain. The jagged elbows of the dirty straw strewn about the stable
dig into her skin. They ooze blood from web-thin capillaries.
Gasps of pain gust from Mary's lips and still the night stretches on. Tears carve
watery channels in the layers of grime on her cheek.
There are no midwives. Nor a mother's hand to grasp. And yet
Mary's sweet cries rise like luminous strands of praise to the God of Israel.
And it is not a silent night as we have long been fooled into believing.
Blood mingled with straw. Sweat and tears flow in salty slurry like
the weeping children of Abraham in Egypt long ago.
A gasp. A cry. A final heave. Mary collapses against

the wall. Joseph stoops to lift a crying infant—a little boy—
from the squalor of the stable's floor. He wraps the child
in strips of rough, soggy cloth and rests him in a ruinous,
half-rotten
feeding box. Then down, he kneels beside his betrothed and holds
her.
The howling wind outside seems to recognize
the One who set it on its course and it mourns with great
wails of lament. For it knows that which no living mind could ever
conceive. The
Maker of all things has come to be unmade by the very ones He
made.
And creation weeps to welcome her King.

DECEMBER 25 12:23 PM PART THREE

"His name is Jesus," Mary whispers wearily. And she closes her
eyes.
The child's mouth works in and out, perhaps dreaming
of his mother's breast and the warm throb of a loving
heart against his cheek. Or then, perhaps, he dreams of
things beyond the comprehension of man; shining,
melodic, silvery things that we each of us long for with a mighty
ache, yet
have called by other names: Nostalgia, Romance, Beauty, Mystery.
Perhaps this child is these very wonders incarnate; perhaps he is the
missing link
in all we love and profess to cherish; in all we hold most dear. For
this child is not merely a human babe; he is Yahweh,
he is Elohim, the Word in the beginning, the Word by which all
things

have their being, the Word that was with God and is God since
before the dawn of time.

DECEMBER 26 10:44 AM PART FOUR

He is a Warrior King, a Boy Hero, a wise Rabbi, an Offensive Fool.
He is the manna in the wilderness, the serpent on the pole, the water
from the rock, the second Adam, the remnant of Eden, the atoning
Lamb,
a crowning point in Abraham's starry line, the fulfillment of David's
royal
legacy, he is hope for the Gentile, promise for the Jew, and Lord of all.
He is Messiah, Emmanuel, Son of Man, Man of Sorrows, Alpha and
Omega,
Bread of Life, Good Shepherd, Savior, Servant, Author, Redeemer,
Maker,
Teacher, Mediator. He is the Lion of Judah, the Bridegroom and
Cornerstone,
King of Kings, Lord of Lords, Prince of Peace, Way, Truth, Life,
he is the great I AM, El-Shaddai, Adonai-Jehovah, myth become fact,
Jesus the Christ. And yet now He sleeps! Not in
the opulence of a royal bedchamber, heralded by criers and
waited upon by slaves, but rather in a filthy stable, surrounded by
barn animals and nursed by a shivering, disheveled virgin girl. This is
his upside-down kingdom, and thus, though he made it all, he
comes to die.
Yet on this night in Israel, he wails and tests his stubby fingers and
watches
the moon set. This is Messiah. The bones of the earth tremble.

DECEMBER 27 9:54 AM

I was sitting near the water as the sank low behind the silver sea.
And a fierce
pastel of clouds were torn asunder like a stricken braid of leaves.
And the pearl-pale
sky of summer breathed a shining strand of fire to melt the waves.
And like a bloody
flower unrisen, the dying embers glisten, from the groaning of
their prison, they're straining now to listen as a chorus in the
heights begins to play.

DECEMBER 28 10:18 AM

You tell the little children to come, but I hold back. I watch, terrified,
as the other children run to you. You rest a hand on each of their
heads, whispering
blessings to them as they gaze up at you with fearless, eager faces.
But I know how wretched my own heart is; I weep bitterly, but I
know you'll see my
brokenness when I come. And I'm scared that the eyes of Love itself
will look upon me and turn away in disgust.

DECEMBER 29 10:54 AM

I sit in the heart of a sky rise, surrounded by frowning titans of
glass and stone.
There's a sort of beauty in this man-made skyline, but it's so mod-
ern, so recent
compared to the vast, blue expanse of Lake Michigan stretching
away beyond

the city. Or even to the ground these babels were built upon; the lake and the ground
were here when Christ walked upon Galilee's foaming deeps,
yet we call this place 'Chicago' as if it was ever ours to name.

DECEMBER 30 1:08 PM

We have gathered here among a web of words, wanderers converging
within a sanctuary of sentences. The saint inside us seeks the truest Word,
the child inside us yearns to scramble upon language as if it were
a great, climbing tree. Saints and children, together we come
to hear again the sacred story, to sing again the ancient song.

DECEMBER 31 6:01 PM

After this year of seeking the secret fire of stillness, of voyaging
upon high, wild-strewn seas, of soaring mightily into the halls of heaven
and descending even unto the gateway of hell, my heart yet sings; sings
for joys I have yet to know, sings for a world still woven through
with rumbling echoes of Eden, sings in this cathedral of creation.
I sing a song of stillness for the stillness I have found,
a stillness rising up and in, a stillness ever heavenbound.
So come, ye pilgrim, come and drink of Christ, incarnate stillness raised.
Come wherever thou mayst roam, come to this place where every whisper is praise.

www.ingramcontent.com/pod-product-compliance
Lightning Source LLC
LaVergne TN
LVHW012333100826
845148LV00017B/2134

* 9 7 9 8 3 8 5 2 7 2 4 6 4 *